Communicating
in Business English

Bob Dignen

Compass
Publishing

Communicating in Business English
Bob Dignen

© 2003 published by Compass Publishing Inc.

109 Van Dyke Place
Guilderland, NY 12084
USA

First published 1998 & 1999
© Asia Pacific Press Holdings Ltd 1999 & 2000

Acquisitions Editor: Casey D. Malarcher
Cover / Interior Design: Design Plus

http: // www.compasspub.com
email: info@compasspub.com

ISBN: 978-1-932222-17-3

24 25 26 27 28 29 30
15 14 13 12

Contents...

Introduction

Communicating in Business English is designed for people interested in developing their communication skills for business. The focus of this book is on functional English that people need to communicate within various business environments.

The six chapters in *Communicating in Business English* include the following business related situations: making telephone calls, giving presentations, participating in meetings, talking with business contacts, negotiating agreements, and writing business documents. Each chapter consists of fourteen lessons of two pages each: an explanation page and an exercise page.

The explanation page for each lesson includes a key vocabulary list along the left side of the page. These lists are divided into parts of speech to aid readers in learning and reviewing vocabulary. The rest of the explanation page contains information related to a particular aspect of the chapter's thematic situation. Typically, chapters begin with an overview of the situation, followed by in-depth discussion of various parts of the situation, cross-cultural tips for effective communication, and golden rules for successfully getting the job done.

The exercise page for each lesson begins with a short dialog/cloze exercise. Through the dialogs, readers will be able to see how various words and phrases from the explanation page fit together in conversation. The dialogs typically follow a single story-line exemplifying the situation of the chapter and are available in recorded form. Additional exercises in each lesson allow readers to practice using vocabulary and sentence structures from the lessons through a variety of methods. Answers for all of the exercises are provided at the back of the book.

It is not necessary for readers to go through this book strictly in the order the chapters are presented. However, it is suggested readers work through all fourteen lessons in a chapter in order to help them follow the flow of the chapter's situation. This will also allow readers to work through the chapter's dialog exercises in order to aid comprehension.

By using *Communicating in Business English*, readers will develop a firm foundation of business English skills to help them communicate and function in a wide range of business situations.

With the additional resources provided by EnglishCentral, ***Communicating in Business English*** comes alive for students wishing to strengthen their language skills as well as hone their ability to communicate in the international business world.

Additional Features of EnglishCentral:

- **Interactive Speaking Practice** - Proprietary speech assessment technology "listens" to learners' speech and scores it based on pronunciation and syntax. Feedback is instantaneous, motivating learners to keep practicing. Learners can compare their speech with native speakers at the word or line level.

- **Listening Comprehension Features** - Captioning and clickable transcripts with in-context definitions provide support for listening comprehension and vocabulary building. Any line can be paused and played back in "slow speak" mode for easier comprehension.

- **Goals & Achievements** - Learners earn points based on how well they speak each dialogue of ***Communicating in Business English***, and can compare their achievements with anyone else in the EnglishCentral community.

- **Teacher Tools** - For teachers, EnglishCentral provides tools to track student learning and speaking progress, including how many passages students study, how many lines they have spoken, and the points they have earned from their speaking practice.

CHAPTER 1

English for the Telephone

1. What makes a good telephone call?

Vocabulary

NOUNS
antenna
battery
code
cold call
connection
dial tone
display
extension
greeting
objective
reason
result
signal
small talk
subscriber
teleconference
touch pad
voice mail

VERBS
call collect
check
communicate
confirm
greet
identify
plan
prepare
recharge
reverse
charge

ADJECTIVES
available
busy
long distance
positive

ADVERBS
politely
positively

A checklist

Before the call
Prepare well before you call.
Plan what you want to say.
Prepare answers to possible questions.
Send an e-mail before the call, if necessary.
Have all information available.

Beginning the call
Make a greeting and identify yourself clearly.
Ask for connection to the person you want to speak to.
After connection, greet the person.
Small talk *
Give a reason for the call.

During the call
Create a positive atmosphere.
Communicate your objective clearly.
Listen — make sure you understand.
Check — make sure the other person understands you.

Ending the call
Confirm the result of the call.
End politely and positively.

*See page 32, Cross Cultural Tips

The first thing I wanted to talk about is the budget.

Prepare your telephone call in advance.

Recharging the battery.

receiver

antenna

display

touch pad

phone

cellular phone

subscriber

BASIC TERMS

Equipment	People	Services
Phone	Caller	Directory assistance
Receiver	Subscriber	Voice mail
Cellular (mobile) phone	Switchboard operator	
Display		
Handset		
Hands-free kit		
Teleconference facilities		
Battery		

Can I interest you in some low-priced English dictionaries?

Cold call—selling

Numbers
Local
National
International code
Extension
Work number
Home number

Calls
A cold call
An international call
A local call
A conference call
A long distance call

Tones
Dial tone
Busy signal
Number not in service

When the receiver pays = **to reverse** the charges - U.K.
to make a collect call - U.S.A.

Fill in the blanks. Listen and check.

plan	small talk	cold call	busy signal

Linda: Would it be possible to get some tips from you for calling customer

Mark: Sure. I can show you the _____ I use when I call custome

Linda: You prepare everything you're going to say before you call?

Mark: No, but I have an outline I follow for calls. If it is a _____, I
customer and identify myself. Then I tell them the reason for my c

Linda: You don't start the conversation with _____?

Mark: No. I get to the point by politely asking if they are interested. It saves

Linda: Do you ever leave messages for people on their voice mail?

Mark: Not usually. And if I get a _____, I call that person again later in the

V O C A B U L A R Y

Circle the word that does not belong in each group.

1. antenna   dial tone   display   touch pad

2. communicate   listen   redial   speak

3. busy signal   call waiting   caller ID   voice mail

4. access code   extension   phone number   zip code

5. check   confirm   greet   repeat

P R A C T I C E

Choose the best word to complete the sentence.

1. He is not _____ to come to the phone right now.
   a. available   b. positive   c. possible   d. necessary

2. I think this phone is broken. I didn't hear a _____ when I picked it up.
   a. dial tone   b. greeting   c. subscriber   d. touch pad

3. My cell phone battery is low, so I should _____ it.
   a. confirm   b. identify   c. recharge   d. reverse

4. The manager requested a _____ with the branch office in Mexico.
   a. battery   b. cold call   c. small talk   d. teleconference

5. Is it possible to make _____ calls from the phones in the office?
   a. available   b. busy   c. positive   d. long distance

2. Making a Call

A communication story

NOUNS
dial tone
directory
message
number
operator
receiver
star key

VERBS
answer
call
call back
connect
dial
get
get through
hang up
know
leave
look up
offer
pick up
press
put down
return
ring
speak with
take down
transfer

ADJECTIVES
automated

ADVERBS
angrily

You want to **call** Bob. ➤ You **don't know his number.** ➤ You **look up the number** in the telephone directory. ➤ You **pick up the receiver.** ➤ You listen for the **dial tone.** ➤ You **dial the number.** ➤ The telephone **rings.** ➤ The **switchboard operator answers.** ➤ The **operator transfers your call.** ➤ Peter **picks up the phone.** ➤ You **get through.** ➤ Peter **answers** the phone. ➤ You ask **to speak with Bob.** ➤ Bob is **sick.** ➤ You **leave** a message asking Bob to **call you back.** ➤ Peter **takes down** the message. ➤ You **thank Peter for his help** and say goodbye. ➤ You **put the phone down.** ➤ You wait for Bob to **return your call.** ➤ Bob **calls you back** later. ➤ Your company **has automated dialing.** ➤ Bob **presses the**

star key to connect to your department. ➤ Your colleague **takes the call** as you are out of the office. ➤ Your colleague offers to **take a message** but Bob **hangs up** angrily! ➤ You never **get** another **call** from Bob.

Key vocabulary

The caller
To phone
To give someone a call
To call / call someone up
To make a (phone) call to ...

Person called
To receive a call
To get a call
To have a call

The phone call
A telephone call
A call

> Could you speak up? The reception is very poor.

Communication in the 21st century

D I A L O G  http://access.englishcentral.com/compass/makingacall

Fill in the blanks. Listen and check.

connect	directory	dial tone	transfer

Mark: These new phones are too fancy. I don't know how to use them.

Linda: It's easy. Watch. First, pick up the receiver.

Mark: I don't hear a _____.

Linda: You have to press the number of the person you want to speak with first. Or if you want to dial out of the office, press the number 9.

Mark: Is there a _____ somewhere so I can look up people's extension numbers?

Linda: They're on this list. These numbers _____ you to other desks in the office.

Mark: And when the phone rings, I answer it by pressing the flashing light?

Linda: Right. And you can _____ a call by pressing hold and the extension number.

V O C A B U L A R Y

Label the phone using the words below.

cord	hold button	pound key	receiver	star key

1. _____

2. _____

3. _____

5. _____

4. _____

P R A C T I C E

Fill in the blanks with the correct word.

back	down	through	up	with

1. He tried to get _____ to the main office all morning, but the line was busy.

2. If he is not in the office right now, I'll just call _____ later this afternoon.

3. Let me get a pen so I can take _____ your new number.

4. May I speak _____ whoever is in charge of customer accounts?

5. She forget the number, so she had to look it _____.

3. Switchboard speaking!

Vocabulary

NOUNS
caller
colleague
connection
line
meeting
message
moment
name
number
vacation

VERBS
answer
apologize
ask
call
call back
check
connect
have
hold
identify
leave
put through
speak
transfer

ADJECTIVES
afraid
sick
sorry

Identifying your company/department

Good morning. Lake Technology.
Personnel Department.

Asking about the purpose

How can I help you?
What is it in regard to?
What can I do for you?
Who would you like to speak to?

Identifying the caller

I'm sorry, could I have your name (again), please?
Who's calling, please?

Connecting

One moment, please.
I'll check if he's in his office.

Apologies

I'm afraid
   – the line is busy.
   – he's on the other line.
   – he's in a meeting (at the moment).
   – she's out of the office today.
   – he's on vacation.
He'll be back soon/later this afternoon.
She won't be back until this afternoon.

No connection

Do you want to hold?
Would you like to speak to his colleague?
Can I take a message?
Would you like to leave a message?
Would you like him to call you back?
Does she have your number?

Making the connection

Just a moment. I'm putting you through, now.
I'll connect you now.

Answering a call — identifying yourself

Good morning. Bob Adams (speaking).
This is Bob Adams.
This is he/she.

D I A L O G
 http://access.englishcentral.com/compass/switchboardspeaking

Fill in the blanks. Listen and check.

meeting	speak	call you back	leave

Operator: Good afternoon. JP&B Associates. How can I help you?

Linda: I'd like to _____ with Larry Smith, please.

Operator: Please hold while I put your call through ... I'm sorry. I'm afraid Mr. Smith is out of the office at the moment. Would you like to _____ a message?

Linda: I wanted to check to make sure he remembered our _____ tomorrow.

Operator: If you leave your name and number, I'll ask him to _____ when he gets in.

Linda: Certainly. My name is Linda Strait ...

V O C A B U L A R Y

Complete the definitions with a word from the Vocabulary list.

1. A person you work with is also called your_____.

2. If the phone is ringing and you pick it up, it means you _____ it.

3. The phone is busy when another caller is already on the _____.

4. To tell someone your name is to _____ yourself.

5. When you apologize, you say that you are _____.

P R A C T I C E

Match the question with the correct response.

1. Can I help you?

2. Could I have your name, please?

3. Would you like to leave a message?

4. Could I transfer you to anyone else?

5. Does she have your number?

a. I'll give it to you just in case she doesn't.

b. I would like to speak with Steve Cross.

c. No, he's the only one who can help me.

d. It's Debra Wilson.

e. No, I'll call back a little later.

4. Opening a call

NOUNS
apple
call
connection
day
echo
extension
introduction
jacket
pronunciation
reason
summer
tango
teacher
whiskey
window
yourself

VERBS
ask
check
give
go
make
pronounce

ADJECTIVES
American
British
indigo
yellow

Making the call — identifying yourself

Hello, this is ....
My name is ....
This is ... speaking.
Hi, Bob. It's John here.

My name is Bond, John Bond.

Asking for connection

I'd like to speak to ....
Could/Can/May I speak to ....
Could you put me through to ....
Extension 361, please.

Giving more details

It's in connection with ....
It's about ....

Could I speak to someone in the Transportation Department, please?

Checking after connection

Is this Maria/the Personnel Department?
Are you the person responsible for ...?

Reason for calling

I'm calling to ....
The reason I called is to ....
I'm calling about ....

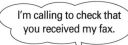

I'm calling to check that you received my fax.

Shall I spell my name?

The alphabet — introduction to pronunciation							Key sounds — a guide
/ei/	/iː/	/e/	/uː/	/ai/	/ɑːr/	/ou/	**A** for Apple/Alpha
A	B	F	Q	I	R	O	**D** as in Day/Delta
H	C	L	U	Y			**E** for Edward/Echo
J	D	M					**G** as in Go/Golf
K	E	N					**I** for Into/Indigo
	G	S					**J** as in Jacket/Juliet
	P	X					**R** for Robert/Romeo
	T						**S** as in Summer/Sierra
	V						**T** for Teacher/Tango

Z is pronounced 'zee' in American English and 'zed' in British English.

W as in Window/Whiskey
Y for Yes/Yellow

D I A L O G http://access.englishcentral.com/compass/openingacall

Fill in the blanks. Listen and check.

indigo	check	reason	give

Linda: My name is Linda Strait. Is Ms. Brown in?
Secretary: May I ask the _____ of your call?
Linda: Ms. Brown asked me to _____ the status of her order with us.
Secretary: Ms. Brown is not at her desk at the moment. If you _____ me your name and number, I can ask her to call you back.
Linda: Alright. My name is Linda Strait. My last name is spelled "S" as in summer, "T" as in teacher, "R" like Robert, "A" apple, "I" like _____, "T" teacher.
Secretary: I'll give her the message, Ms. Strait.

V O C A B U L A R Y

Choose the best word to match the meaning of the underlined words.

1. The CEO of the company is <u>from England</u>.

   a. American   b. British   c. Foreign   d. Indigo

2. I'm not sure how to correctly <u>say</u> your name.

   a. check   b. give   c. go   d. pronounce

3. We must have a bad connection because I can hear a <u>repeating noise</u> on the line.

   a. echo   b. introduction   c. reason   d. window

4. You should wear a <u>light coat</u> today. It's a little cool outside.

   a. extension   b. jacket   c. tango   d. whiskey

5. It's hard to believe you did all this work <u>alone</u>.

   a. alpha   b. delta   c. yellow   d. yourself

P R A C T I C E

Fill in the blanks with the correct word from the "key sounds" guide.

My name spelled . . .

1. E as in _____, A as in _____, R as in _____, L as in lemon.
2. J like _____, E like _____, R like _____, R like _____, Y like _____.
3. S as in _____, A like _____, G as in _____, E like _____.
4. Y like _____, V like violin, E as in _____, S as in _____.
5. D as in _____, A as in _____, W like _____, N like Nancy.

5. Receiving and taking messages

Vocabulary

NOUNS
action
address
area code
contact number
date
digit
name
switchboard
zero

VERBS
call back
go ahead
go over
make sure
read back
repeat
spell
take
tell
write down

ADJECTIVES
ready
right

The switchboard

Names and addresses
Can I have your name again?
Could you spell that for me?

Numbers
Can I have your number?
What's the area/country code?
Is that your mobile/your office?

Noting and responding
I'd better write this down.
 Just a moment. OK. Ready.
Let me get a pen. OK. Go ahead.

Checking
Could you go over that again, please?
Let me just repeat that for you.
Should I read that back, just to check?

Don't worry!
I'll make sure she gets the message.
I'll tell him you called.
I'll get him to call you as soon as he
 gets back to the office.

> **Check!**
> **TAKING MESSAGES**
> Name of caller:
> Date and time of call:
> Message:
> Action to be taken:
> Contact number:
> Call taken by:

The caller

The message
Could you tell him/her I called?
Could you ask her to call me back?
Please tell him that I'll call back.

Spelling
It's Dignen. Should I spell that for you?
Yes, it's Gere. G-E-R-E.

Numbers
Yes, it's 013-794-2863.
[See note below]
That's my cellular.

Replies
Of course.
OK. Yes, that's right.
Please.

Thanks
Thank you very much.
Could I just have your name?
Thank you. Goodbye.

Note
Telephone numbers are usually said digit by digit. However, there are other ways. For instance, "2246" can be said like "double two-four-six" or "twenty-two, forty-six." The number "O" can be pronounced "oh," or "zero."

Fill in the blanks. Listen and check.

Go ahead	number	tell	make sure

Mark: Linda is not here right now. Can I take a message?

Sam: This is her husband. Could you ask her to call me? I'm at my office, but she needs to call me at extension _____ 204.

Mark: I'd better write this down. Hold on a moment while I find a pen. OK. _____.

Sam: My office number is 471-3006. Extension 204.

Mark: Let me repeat that back to _____ I got it. 471-3006 and extension 204.

Sam: That's right.

Mark: I'll _____ her to call you as soon as she gets back to the office.

Sam: Thank you very much.

V O C A B U L A R Y

Fill in the blanks on the following phone message using the words below.

action	date	message	name

_____: May 2, 2003

_____: Alice White

Time: 3:45 PM

_____: wants to reschedule meeting

_____: (✓) please call   ( ) will call again

P R A C T I C E

Put the following sentences in logical order (a=first, e=last).

_____ **1.** Can you tell me the area code again, please?

_____ **2.** He is not in the office at the moment.

_____ **3.** I'll make sure he gets the message. Goodbye.

_____ **4.** If you leave your name and contact number, I'll have him call you.

_____ **5.** Thank you for calling TestPro. May I help you?

6. Structuring a call

NOUNS
logistics
purpose
structure

VERBS
arrange
check
confirm
deal with
decide
deflect
discuss
explain
get back to
handle
inform
leave to
organize
structure
talk about

ADVERBS
carefully
finally
first
second

The purpose

I'm calling about ....
Peter asked me to call you to organize ....
I would like to discuss ....
We need to organize ....
We have to arrange ....

Structure

There are three things I would like to talk about.
First, I want to discuss ....
Second, ...
Finally, ...
Another thing is ....

Check

Is that OK with you?
Is this a good time to talk about this?
Do you have time right now?

Deciding

OK. Then we have decided to ....
Right. Then I will ....
I will leave this to you.
So, you're going to handle this. OK?
Should I deal with the logistics?

Deflecting

Can we deal with that another time?
I'll have to get back to you about ....

Further action

Could you send me an e-mail to confirm that?
Would you please inform Peter?

Final check

Is there anything else?
Is that everything / all?

I'm calling to arrange a meeting for next week.

Explain why you are calling.

There are a few things I would like to discuss.

Explain the subject of the call.

Is there anything else?

Telephoning tip
Plan what you want to say carefully before you call!

D I A L O G http://access.englishcentral.com/compass/structuringacall

Fill in the blanks. Listen and check.

get back to you	organize	confirm	leave it to

Linda: I'm calling to _____ that I've received your order by fax. However, we need to discuss the payment schedule for your order.

Frank: Can I _____ about this? I don't usually deal with payments, and the person who usually handles them is out to lunch.

Linda: I see. Would you like me to explain the payment options to that person?

Frank: I think we talked about that when we met here in my office. I think you can _____ me to inform her of the payment options.

Linda: When you have decided on the option you'd like to use, please call me back.

Frank: I'll do that. Is there anything else we need to discuss regarding our order?

Linda: No. Once we _____ the payment schedule, everything will be set.

V O C A B U L A R Y

Match the words that mean the same.

1. confirm	**a.** arrange
2. get back to	**b.** check
3. handle	**c.** deal with
4. organize	**d.** discuss
5. talk about	**e.** contact again

P R A C T I C E

Write the phrase to describe what each sentence is doing.

checking	deflecting	deciding	ending	telling the purpose

1. "Can I get back to you about that later?" _____

2. "Do you have a few minutes to talk?" _____

3. "I'm calling to dicuss your order." _____

4. "OK. I'll take care of that." _____

5. "Thanks for your time. Bye." _____

7. Transferring information

NOUNS
information
mistake
spelling

VERBS
cancel
catch
check
confirm
correct
excuse
follow
go ahead
go over
hear
listen
mean
pardon
read back
respond
spell
start

ADJECTIVES
correct
important
right

ADVERBS
exactly
quite

Starting	Confirming
Ready?	Yes, go ahead.
Have you got a pen?	Yes.

Checking	Confirming
Have you got that?	Yes, you said ....
Could you read that back to me, please?	OK.
OK?	Let me read that back.
Should I repeat that?	Please, yes.

Active listening — responding

OK.   Right.   Got that.

You don't hear

Sorry?
Pardon me?
Excuse me?
I beg your pardon?

I'm sorry, I didn't hear what you said.
I didn't quite catch that.
I didn't catch what you said.

I didn't understand. Could you repeat that, please?
I'm sorry. Could you go over that again, please?

It is not clear

I'm sorry. What do you mean exactly?
I'm sorry. I don't follow. What is 'turnover'?
What do you mean by 'turnover'?

You want to check

Did you say ....
Let me just check. You said ... Is that right?
You said you wanted to cancel the meeting? Is that correct?

Asking for spelling

Would / Could you spell that, please?

Correcting information

Sorry, not the 30th. I said the 13th.
Sorry, that's not quite right.
Sorry, I think that's a mistake. It should be ....

Telephoning tip
Repeat important numbers to check.

D I A L O G http://access.englishcentral.com/compass/transferringinformation

Fill in the blanks. Listen and check.

important	Excuse me	information	read that back

Linda: Could you give Sam a message for me when he gets in? Ready?
Chris: Go ahead.
Linda: His sister Myra is arriving tonight, but I'm tied up at work.
Chris: _____? Could you spell her name for me?
Linda: That's M-Y-R-A. She's on the 7:50 flight from Denver.
Chris: Pardon me. Did you say 7:15?
Linda: No, fifty. Five zero. From Denver. It's very _____ that he get this _____ and there are not any mistakes. Can you _____ to me, please?
Chris: OK. Myra is arriving tonight from Denver at 7:50. I'll give him the message.

V O C A B U L A R Y

Match the sentences/questions with the same meaning.

1. Got it?   a. Excuse me?

2. I didn't quite follow that.   b. I think you made a mistake.

3. Pardon me?   c. OK?

4. That's not quite right.   d. So, just to check, that's tomorrow.

5. You said tomorrow, right?   e. I'm not sure what you mean by that.

P R A C T I C E

Find a verb in the Vocabulary list that has the same meaning as the underlined words.

1. He planned to <u>begin</u> calling customers after lunch. _____

2. It was hard for me to <u>understand</u> every word she said over the phone. _____

3. Please <u>review</u> the information I sent and call me if you have questions. _____

4. She called the airline to <u>verify</u> her ticket. _____

5. You should <u>say something</u> to show you are paying attention to the caller. _____

8. Communication difficulties

Vocabulary

NOUNS
answer
battery
line
problem

VERBS
call right back
contact
cut off
get a hold of
hang up
have the wrong
  number
lose
reach
speak up
transfer back

ADJECTIVES
busy
general
in service
noisy
technical
terrible
wrong

ADVERBS
hardly
nearly

Problems

General
Just a minute. Let me get a pen.
The line is busy.
There's no answer.
I can't contact / get a hold of Peter!

The line is busy.

There's no answer.

Technical
The number is not in service.
We were cut off.

They were cut off!

There is a really bad echo. I'll call you back.

HELLO HELLO HELLO

Sound
I can hardly hear you.
Can you speak up?
It's very noisy here.
Can you speak up a little, please?
It's a terrible / bad line.
Can you hear me?

I'm losing you.

Cellular phones
My battery is nearly out.
I'm losing you. I'm going into a tunnel.
There are some problems with the net.

To the operator
I'm having problems with a New York number.
Could you check the line, please?

Wrong numbers

I'm sorry, I think you have the wrong number.
I think I have the wrong number.
  Is this 019-945-5677?
I'm afraid you've reached sales.
  I'll try and transfer you back to the switchboard.

I think you've got the wrong number.

Call back

I'll call you right back.
Hang up and I'll try again.
Talk to you in a moment.

Communication problems.

D I A L O G http://access.englishcentral.com/compass/communicationdifficulties

Fill in the blanks. Listen and check.

hang up	hardly	busy	wrong number

Diane: Hi, Linda? I've been calling all morning, but the line has been _____.
Linda: Hello? Can you speak up? I can _____ hear you. Who is calling, please?
Diane: It's Diane! Can you hear me now?
Linda: Hi, Diane! What's wrong with this phone line? Is your battery dying?
Diane: It's not my cell phone. This line is terrible. Let me _____ and call you right back.
[Both hang up. Diane dials again.]
Woman: Hello?
Diane: Who is this? Is this Linda?
Woman: There's no Linda here. I think you have the _____.

V O C A B U L A R Y

Match the problem with the sentence to describe it.

1. another caller on line   **a.** I'm sorry. The line is busy.

2. company went out of business   **b.** Speak up! I can hardly hear you!

3. volume is too low   **c.** The number is no longer in service.

4. cell phone beyond service range   **d.** There is nobody here by that name.

5. wrong number   **e.** The signal is too weak. Call me later.

P R A C T I C E

Choose the best word to complete the sentence.

1. I don't know why, but we were suddenly _____ in the middle of our conversation.
    a. cut off   b. lost   c. reached   d. spoken

2. You can _____ customer service by dialing "1" now.
    a. hang up   b. lose   c. reach   d. transfer

3. It's too _____ to talk in this restaurant. Let me call you back after lunch.
    a. general   b. noisy   c. technical   d. wrong

4. This is outrageous! I've been on hold for _____ ten minutes!
    a. exactly   b. hardly   c. finally   d. nearly

5. Due to a _____ problem, the office phones will not be working for the next hour.
    a. busy   b. important   c. technical   d. communication

9. Calling back

NOUNS
excuse
reason
subject
thanks
time

VERBS
call back
get back to
go over
open
restart
return
talk
talk about
thank

ADJECTIVES
alright
available
better

ADVERBS
actually

Opening

I'm returning your call.
My secretary said you called.
I got your message.
Thanks for calling earlier.

Aha, Mr. Smith. I'm returning your call. My secretary said you rang.

Thanking

Thanks for calling back.
Thanks for getting back to me so soon.

Reason for call

The reason I called earlier was that ....
What I wanted to talk about was ....
I called earlier to ....

Timing

Is this a good time to talk?
Do you have time now to ...?
Do you have the information with you?
Can we go over the figures now?
Do you have a few minutes to talk about this now?

Is this a good time to talk?

Actually, I'm in a meeting right now. Can I call you back?

Excuses

Actually, I'm in a meeting right now.
I'm afraid I'm on the other line.
I was just on my way to a meeting.

Call back

I'll call you back.
Let me call you back.
Can I call you back in five minutes?

Close

Talk to you soon/again.

Can you hear me now?

Yes, much better.

Calling back — restarting

This is Peter returning your call.
Hello again. It's Peter.
Is the line any better?
Can you hear me alright now?

Back to the subject

The reason I called was ....
OK. Where were we?
As I was saying ....

D I A L O G   http://access.englishcentral.com/compass/callingback

Fill in the blanks. Listen and check.

getting back to	returning	available	call you back

Linda: This is Linda. I got a message you called, so I'm _____ your call.

Frank: Hi, Linda. Thanks for _____ me so soon. The reason I called you was to check and see if our order has been shipped.

Linda: Yes, it was shipped yesterday.

Frank: Great! I'll need to check the information later.

Linda: If you like, I can go over the invoice with you now. Are you _____ now to talk about it?

Frank: Actually I have an appointment. Is it alright if I _____ in an hour?

Linda: No problem. Talk to you soon.

Frank: Thanks. Bye.

V O C A B U L A R Y

Label what each person is doing by using the following words.

opening	thanking	giving a reason	giving an excuse	restarting

1. As I was saying, Friday is not a good day for me. _____

2. I got a message that you called. _____

3. I'm on the other line at the moment, so I can't really talk. _____

4. Thanks for calling me back. _____

5. I wanted to talk to you about playing golf on Friday. _____

P R A C T I C E

Put the following sentences in logical order (1=first, 5=last).

_____ **Man:** Alright. I'll talk to you this afternoon.

_____ **Woman:** I have a meeting in ten minutes. This afternoon is better for me.

_____ **Woman:** Oh, yes. Thanks for getting back to me so quickly.

_____ **Man:** I just received a message that you called me.

_____ **Man:** I was glad you called. Do you have a few minutes to talk now?

10. Making appointments

Vocabulary

NOUNS
agenda
appointment
calendar
diary
planner
schedule

VERBS
check
come up
expect
manage
meet
move forward
move up
pick up
postpone
rearrange
reschedule
schedule
sound
suit

ADJECTIVES
best
convenient
fine
free
ideal
nice

Arranging a meeting	Responses
Can we schedule a meeting?	Yes, of course.
Can we have a meeting next month?	Sure.
Would you like to meet for lunch?	That would be nice.
Let me check my calendar.	

Agreeing on a time

Could you manage sometime next week?
When would be best for you?
When is good for you?
Are you free on ...?
I'm free on Tuesday. Is that convenient for you?
How would Tuesday suit you?
How does Tuesday sound?
Shall we say 2 o'clock?

Language Difference

UK	USA
Diary	Calendar
Bus timetable	Bus schedule

Note
1. Agenda is for meetings.
2. For project planning we use 'schedule' or 'planner' in both British and US English.

Canceling

Can we change our appointment time? Something has come up. I have to ....
Could we reschedule / rearrange it for Friday?
Could we make it Friday instead?
Could we postpone it until Saturday?
Could we move it up / forward to Monday?

Saying 'Yes'

Yes, I can make Tuesday.
OK. Tuesday would be fine.
Great. Tuesday is good for me.

Saying 'No'

I'm afraid I have a meeting.
Actually, I'm busy on Tuesday.
That's not ideal, I'm afraid.
I can't make it on Tuesday, sorry.

Unfortunately, I have to cancel our meeting on Tuesday.

Place

Where shall we have the meeting? Your office or mine?
I'll come to your office if you like.

Confirming

OK. So, I will expect you at my office at 10, then.
OK, I'll see you on Tuesday at 10 o'clock in my office.
I'll confirm that by e-mail.

I'll see you on Friday, then.

Confirm the arrangement at the end of the call.

Organization

Someone will meet you at the airport.
John will pick you up at your hotel and bring you to the office.
If you're driving, there's a parking lot in front of the main building.
Just ask for me at the reception desk.

http://access.englishcentral.com/compass/makingappointments

Fill in the blanks. Listen and check.

schedule	ideal	convenient	planner

Mary: When would you like to _____ our meeting?
Linda: When would be best for you?
Mary: I'm free on Wednesday afternoon. Is that day _____ for you?
Linda: Could we make it Thursday morning instead?
Mary: Let me check my _____. Yes, Thursday morning is fine. What time?
Linda: How does 10:00 sound?
Mary: 10:00 is _____ for me. I'll expect you Thursday morning at ten.
Linda: Great! See you then.

VOCABULARY

Match each word with the correct meaning.

1. agenda
2. appointment
3. calendar
4. planner
5. schedule

a. the planned times and events for a day, week, etc.
b. a record showing weekly or monthly appointments
c. the planned topics or tasks for a meeting
d. an arranged meeting
e. the year divided into months, weeks, and days

PRACTICE

Fill in the blanks in the following planner.

check	meet	pick up	postponed	reschedule

September 27, 2003

Tuesday

9:00   _____ with Chicago branch about last week's shipment

10:00   _____ Ms. Hooper to discuss banquet

11:00   call James to _____ bowling night

12:00   _____ suit from dry cleaners

1:00   budget meeting — _____ until later date

11. Complaining

NOUNS
complaint
error
fault
full responsibility
inconvenience
manual
oversight
quality
reason
replacement

VERBS
accept
apologize
assure
attend to
blame
cancel
damage
deal with
do about
promise
receive
repair
request

ADJECTIVES
acceptable
clerical
unacceptable

ADVERBS
as...as possible
immediately

The complaint

The problem
Excuse me, but we expected delivery ....
I'm sorry but you promised ....
You said that I would have ....
We haven't received ... yet.
   It's now three weeks late.

The goods are not damaged. However, there is a quality problem.

SOCCER CLUB

Request action
Please could you ... as soon as possible?
If you don't repair it immediately,
   we will have to cancel the order.
What are you going to do about it?

Accepting action
OK. That's fine.
OK. That will do.
OK. That will have to do.

Reject Action
I'm sorry but ....
That's unacceptable.
I'm afraid we can't accept that.

Handling the complaint

Ask for information
What is the problem exactly?
Could you explain exactly what the problem is?

Could you tell me the other number?

Get information first.

Saying sorry
I see. We're very sorry about that.
Again, I do apologize.

Explaining the reason for the problem
I'm afraid that we can't/couldn't ....
The reason is that ....
The problem was caused by ....
It was a clerical computer error.
It was an oversight on our part.

A promise of action [will]
I'll deal with it/attend to it/send an engineer immediately.
I'll find/arrange a replacement right away.
Is that acceptable?/Is that OK?

According to my records, you ordered 30, not 300.

Your fault
It's our fault. We accept full responsibility.
We are to blame. We should have .... (repaired it yesterday.)

Explaining

Their fault
I'm sorry but you didn't inform us that you wanted manuals.

Close
I apologize once again. We are very sorry about this.
I apologize for any inconvenience caused. It won't happen again, I assure you.

D I A L O G http://access.englishcentral.com/compass/complaining

Fill in the blanks. Listen and check.

inconvenience	apologize	immediately	oversight

Sam: Is this Pizza House? We ordered a pizza over an hour ago!

Employee: I _____ for that, sir. Can I get your name?

Sam: It's Sam Strait.

Employee: I'm sorry, Mr. Strait, but I can't find your order on our computer.

Sam: What?

Employee: I think there was an error. By some _____, your order was never recorded. I don't know who is to blame for this. Do you know who took the order?

Sam: No, I can't remember. This kind of service is totally unacceptable.

Employee: I assure you, Mr. Strait, this kind of thing rarely happens. We'll get a pizza to your house _____. We're very sorry for the _____.

V O C A B U L A R Y

Find a verb in the Vocabulary list with the same meaning. Write the verb in the blank.

1. accept _____

2. break or harm _____

3. fix _____

4. guarantee _____

5. ask for _____

P R A C T I C E

Correct the mistake in each of the following sentences.

1. I have not receive the pizza I ordered two hours ago!

2. Send someone to fix it as soon possible!

3. She thought the service was unaccepting and asked for her money back.

4. The problem is clearly our fault, so we accept full responsible.

5. We lost your order because of an error clerical.

12. Closing a call

Vocabulary

NOUNS
assistance
confirmation
patience
response
signals

VERBS
close
confirm
go over
leave it at
look forward to
mail
put down
send

ADJECTIVES
efficient
grateful
positive
unprofessional

ADVERBS
alternatively
quickly

Confirmation

So, just to confirm that ....
Let me just go over that again.
So, that's 2 on Friday then.

Promised action

OK. I'll send / mail / organize / phone ....

Closing signals — See 'Tip' below

Anyway .... / Right .... / OK ....
OK. I think that's everything.
Is there anything else?
OK. Well, let's leave it at that for the moment.
OK. I'm sorry but I have to go. The other line is ringing.

Thanking

Thanks for calling (back).
Thank you for your help / patience.
I'm very grateful for your assistance.

Looking forward—positive close

I'll get back to you next week.
I look forward to seeing / meeting / hearing from you next week.
 Nice talking to you.
(**Response**: Me too! Same here! Sounds good!)
Have a good weekend / trip / vacation.

Good-byes

Bye!
Good-bye!
Talk to you again soon!
See you on Monday!

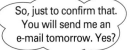

Confirming.

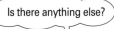

Be efficient when you end a call.

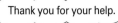

Telephoning tip
Ending telephone calls can be difficult. Calls can easily go on too long.
Alternatively, they can finish too quickly and seem unprofessional. It is important to:
- listen for signals showing that the other person is ready to close that call.
- make signals yourself.
- end on a positive note.
- not put down the receiver too quickly as it may seem rude.

 http://access.englishcentral.com/compass/closingacall

Fill in the blanks. Listen and check.

patience	assistance	go over	leave it at

Linda: Let me quickly just _____ our schedule again. The Thursday morning meeting has been postponed until Monday afternoon at 3 o'clock. Is that right?

Mary: That's right. I'll send you an e-mail Friday to confirm that time again.

Linda: OK. We'll just _____ that unless I hear anything different by Friday.

Mary: I'm sorry about having to change our schedule. Thanks for your _____.

Linda: It's no problem. I'll look forward to seeing you Monday. And if I can be of any more _____, just give me a call.

Mary: I will. See you on Monday.

Linda: Bye.

VOCABULARY

Circle the word that does not belong in each group.

1. close	end	finish	transfer
2. check	organize	go over	confirm
3. aid	assistance	help	receiver
4. hint	sign	signal	trip
5. grateful	inefficient	rude	unprofessional

PRACTICE

Match the sentences with the same meaning.

Formal	Informal
1. I enjoyed talking with you.	a. Talk to you later!
2. Goodbye!	b. Sounds good!
3. Could you go over that again, please?	c. Nice chatting with you.
4. I'm very grateful for all of your help.	d. Thanks a lot.
5. Yes, that would be fine.	e. I didn't catch that. What did you say?

13. Cross-cultural tips/Audio conferencing

Vocabulary

NOUNS
agreement
directness
expectations
friendliness
humor
idiomatic language
indifference
participants
professionalism
punctuality
roll call
silence
small talk

VERBS
clarify
disturb
enable
guarantee
interrupt
notify
repeat
respect
summarize

ADJECTIVES
appropriate
personal
safer
simple
specific

ADVERBS
clearly
concisely
thoroughly

Cultural aspects

- Small talk is expected at the beginning and end of calls in certain countries.
- Repeat important information to guarantee understanding.
- Be patient if there is silence.
  People need time to remember words.
- Clarify if you are not sure.
- Cultures have different rules for the use of first and last names.
  Last names are safer.
- Some people mistake friendliness for unprofessionalism.
- Idiomatic language is more difficult to understand. Keep it simple.
- Silence means different things: agreement to some; indifference, non-understanding to others.
- Punctuality can be very important. Respect expectations.
- Directness can be seen as rude.
- Humor is often very personal and culturally specific.
  Use with caution.

How is the weather?

Small talk may
not be appropriate.

Audio conferencing

Background
Audio conferencing is now very common. It enables people in different locations, often international, to conduct a meeting via the telephone. Use the guidelines below:

Prior to the call
- Notify all participants of the time, date and call-in number for the meeting.

Beginning the call
- Select a location where you will not be disturbed.
- Use a roll call to check participants are present and the lines are clear.

I agree.

Choose a quiet location
for a conference call.

During the call
- Speak clearly and concisely.
- Always state your name before speaking.
- Direct your questions to a named individual.
- Reply to all questions, even if you do not have an immediate answer.
- Do not interrupt.
- Summarize key points of the meeting and agree on action points before ending the call.

International calls

- International calls are costly for the company.
  Plan thoroughly before you call!
- Check the local time of the office you are calling.
- Not everyone speaks English as well as you.
  Send an e-mail if necessary.

DIALOG http://access.englishcentral.com/compass/audioconferencingcrossculturaltips

Fill in the blanks. Listen and check.

| clarify | appropriate | guarantee | directness |

Linda: I'm a little worried about calling Mr. Sanchez in Mexico, Mark. I'm not used to dealing with international clients. Any suggestions?

Mark: I've heard it's good to start with small talk before you get down to business. Americans respect _____ , but other cultures may not.

Linda: Is it _____ for me to call him "Mr." or should I use "senor"?

Mark: I think Mr. is the safer title to use.

Linda: I'm also worried I might not understand his accent.

Mark: I _____ you won't understand everything. But don't worry. Just ask him to repeat or _____ and concisely summarize your notes before you hang up.

VOCABULARY

Match the word with the meaning.

1. agreement

2. friendliness

3. indifference

4. participation

5. professionalism

a. acting well for business

b. being cold and unfeeling

c. being warm and open

d. saying yes

e. taking part

PRACTICE

Complete the sentences by using the following words.

| directness | humor | punctuality | silence | small talk |

1. A culture that believes you should be on time respects _____ .

2. If a person wants you to get to the point, she or he prefers _____ .

3. People who enjoy jokes and laughing have a good sense of _____ .

4. Some cultures communicate without speaking and value _____ .

5. When you chat about the weather, you are using _____ .

14. Golden rules

Practice and rehearse key English phrases.

NOUNS
authority
objectives
respondent
response

VERBS
anticipate
lose control
practice
prepare
pretend
refer to
rehearse
rely on
represent
stand up
waste time

ADJECTIVES
aggressive
agreeable
at hand
clear
complex
essential
polite

ADVERBS
actively
regularly

DO

- plan the call thoroughly. Have clear objectives.
- send an e-mail before you call when necessary.
- anticipate what the other person will say. Prepare your responses.
- have all necessary information at hand.
- refer to this book for essential phrases.
- e-mail ahead to allow the person time to prepare.
- smile when you phone. Be polite and agreeable.
- check that your respondent is free to talk.
- be efficient. You are representing your company.
- use questions to identify key issues.
- be concise. Time is money.
- listen actively. Confirm regularly that you understand.
- stand up. It gives you more authority.
- speak clearly and slowly.
- allow people to finish what they are saying.
- handle complaints politely.
- avoid complex language.
- check that the other person understands.
- take notes during a call. Write them up afterwards.
- send a follow-up e-mail to confirm.
- finish with a positive phrase.

People can hear you smile!

DON'T

- call if you are unprepared.
- assume your respondent is available to talk when you call.
- lose control if someone becomes aggressive.
- forget that you represent the company on the phone.
- waste time.
- pretend to understand.
- assume the person has understood everything.
- interrupt.
- rely on your memory for important details.
- forget to write down important details.
- put the receiver down too quickly. It can seem rude.
- leave your mobile phone switched on in the theater!

D I A L O G http://access.englishcentral.com/compass/goldenrules

Fill in the blanks. Listen and check.

anticipate	representing	aggressive	referred to

Mark: How did your call with Mr. Sanchez go?

Linda: Great! I made a list of objectives before I called and _____ it during the call. That kept us both from wasting time.

Mark: He didn't think you were too _____, did he?

Linda: I don't think so. He was very agreeable and polite during our conversation. One thing I didn't _____ was his sense of humor.

Mark: I'm sure you did a great job _____ the company. You always speak with such authority in meetings.

Linda: And a trick I learned for the phone is to talk standing up. It really works.

V O C A B U L A R Y

Mark each idea as good (DO) or bad (DON'T) according to the Golden Rules.

	DO	DON'T
1. ask if the other person has time to talk	( )	( )
2. talk while the other person is speaking	( )	( )
3. pretend you understand to save time	( )	( )
4. think about what the other person might ask	( )	( )
5. write notes while you are listening	( )	( )

P R A C T I C E

Choose the word with a similar meaning as the underlined word.

1. Do you have a pen and paper <u>close by</u>?

   a. at hand   b. complex   c. on time   d. polite

2. He <u>practiced</u> saying a few phrases in Chinese before he called.

   a. anticipated   b. rehearsed   c. represented   d. wasted

3. I was surprised when she <u>got angry</u> during our conversation.

   a. lost control   b. referred to   c. stood up   d. prepared to

4. Please tell her it is <u>necessary</u> that she call me back this afternoon.

   a. agreeable   b. clear   c. essential   d. polite

5. We thought we could <u>depend on</u> your office to take care of this problem.

   a. refer to   b. rely on   c. stand up   d. waste time

CHAPTER 2

English for Presentations

1. What makes a good presentation?

Vocabulary

NOUNS
aids
attitude
complexity
content
equipment
eye contact
formality
gesture
handout
impact
interest
introduction
involvement
mannerisms
rhythm
sections
structure
visuals
voice
volume

VERBS
adjust
conclude
design
engage
establish
link
promote
provide
summarize

ADJECTIVES
allotted
confident
distracting
maximum
relaxed
relevant

ADVERBS
thoroughly

Checklist

Remember your audience
Establish clear objectives in the introduction
Meet audience expectations with relevant content
Create interest and promote involvement

Involve your audience.

Organize the information
Design an overall structure which is clear
Make sure that the introduction and ending have maximum impact
Link the different sections together
Communicate using the allotted time

Use simple visuals.

Use visuals effectively
Use clear and simple messages
Create impact
Handle visual aids and equipment professionally
Be prepared to provide handouts

Communicate with body language
Maintain a relaxed attitude: remain confident and positive.
Use eye contact to engage your audience
Focus meaning by movement or gesture
Avoid distracting mannerisms

Avoid distracting mannerisms.

Deliver your message
Use your voice effectively: volume, rhythm and pause
Adjust complexity / formality of language to the audience

Prepare thoroughly
Write brief notes to assist
Practice before the real thing

Practice makes perfect.

Use your voice effectively.

Classic presentation organization

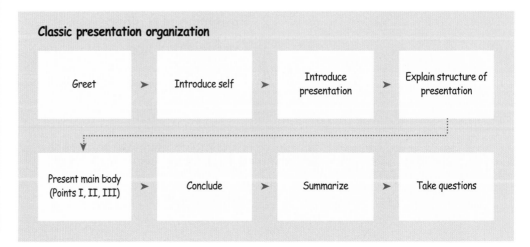

| Greet | ➤ | Introduce self | ➤ | Introduce presentation | ➤ | Explain structure of presentation |

| Present main body (Points I, II, III) | ➤ | Conclude | ➤ | Summarize | ➤ | Take questions |

D I A L O G http://access.englishcentral.com/compass/goodpresentation

Fill in the blanks. Listen and check.

adjust	structure	allotted	eye contact

Mark: Have you had a chance to look over the handout for my presentation?

Linda: Yes, Mark. And I have some questions about the content.

Mark: Really? Do you think I need to _____ the content of the presentation?

Linda: A little. For instance, I don't think the example you give in the introduction is really relevant. And the complexity of the last two sections of the presentation may be too much to explain in the _____ time for this presentation.

Mark: I guess I have a lot more work to do on the _____ of the whole presentation.

Linda: Maybe after you work on it more, you can practice in front of me.

Mark: Great! You can tell me if I use good _____ or have distracting mannerisms.

V O C A B U L A R Y

Match the two parts to make a common phrase used for presentations.

1. audio-visual	**a.** aid
2. confident	**b.** attitude
3. eye	**c.** contact
4. maximum	**d.** equipment
5. visual	**e.** volume

P R A C T I C E

Write the correct label on each note card for the presentation.

conclusion	greeting	introduction	main points	questions

_____
allow audience to
   ask questions

_____
explain background
   of problem

_____
give name and
   welcome audience

_____
reasons why sales fell
new technique
sales results

_____
recommend change
   to new technique

2. Starting

Key Language for Introductions

NOUNS
aim
background
comments
flipchart
greeting
OHP
overhead projector
parts
points
position
sections
springboard
title
topic
whiteboard

VERBS
analyze
convince
divide
examine
move on to
outline
persuade
speak about
split
talk about

ADJECTIVES
brief

Greeting
Good morning/afternoon/evening, ladies and gentlemen.
  Welcome to Ericomm.
Hello/Hi, everyone.

Name and position
Let me just start by introducing myself. My name is Peter Wong.
As some/most of you already know, I am Peter Wong.
I'm in charge of/responsible for production.
I'm the new CEO.

Title/subject
The title/subject/topic of today's presentation/talk is ....
Today, I'd like to speak about ....
 What I'd like to talk about is ....

Objective
The objective of this presentation is to present ....
This talk will act as a springboard for discussion.
The aim today is to give some background about ....

Main parts/outline
I've divided/split my talk into four main parts/sections.
First, what I want to do is give you some background ....
Second/Third, we will look at/move on to ....
Then/Next/After that/Finally, I will speak about/examine ....

Visuals
I will be using the whiteboard and flipchart.
I will be using the overhead projector.

Length of presentation
The presentation will take/last about ... minutes.
I will speak for about ... minutes.
I plan to be brief. About ... minutes.

Questions
If you have any questions, please feel free to interrupt.
Please interrupt me as we go along if you have any questions.
I'd be glad to take any questions at the end of my presentation.

Audience
I know that you have all traveled a long way.
I'm very grateful that you could come today.
It's nice to see so many faces.
I look forward to your comments on this.

Link to start
OK. Let's start with the first point which is....
All right. We can begin by looking at ....

I've divided my talk into four main parts.

Explain the structure.

This presentation will take about three days.

Timing

OK. Let's start with the first point...

Link the different parts of the presentation.

The Classic Introduction — Checklist

- greeting
- name and position
- the title/subject
- the objective
- the main points
- mention visual aids you will use
- time you will take
- when you would like questions
- refer to your audience
- link to first section

Verbs to Explain Objectives

inform	introduce
describe	outline
show	examine
focus on	look at
discuss	persuade
convince	analyze

D I A L O G http://access.englishcentral.com/compass/startingapresentation

Fill in the blanks. Listen and check.

points	brief	outline	title

Mark: Good afternoon, everyone. I'm Mark White, and my position is in the sales department. As you can tell from the _____ of my presentation, the topic I would like to speak about today is methods to get customer feedback about products through informal communication opportunities. First I'd like to _____ my presentation before I jump into the background of how feedback is usually obtained by our company and why informal feedback is useful. As you can see in the handout, there are three main _____ I'll talk about regarding each informal communication opportunity. Let me just write those three points on the whiteboard because I'm going to be referring to them a lot in this presentation. Then we can move on to the _____ outline and introduction ....

V O C A B U L A R Y

Circle the word that does not belong in each group.

1. flip chart   OHP   springboard   whiteboard
2. comment   part   point   section
3. analyze   examine   investigate   persuade
4. discuss   divide   speak about   talk about
5. brief   concise   in-depth   short

P R A C T I C E

Find the correct word in the Vocabulary list to fill in the blanks.

1. The first thing you say in the greeting is your name and _____ in the company.

2. When you tell the audience what the presentation is called, you give the _____.

3. A machine that uses light to show transparent sheets on a screen is an _____.

4. The introduction should be short. In other words, it should be _____.

5. If you are trying to persuade your audience to take action, you are trying to _____ them.

3. Signaling – linking the parts

NOUNS
argument
audience
comments
idea
point
thoughts
questions

VERBS
clarify
come back to
cover
deal with
digress
return to
sequence
signal
turn to

ADVERBS
at this point
clearly

Sequencing ideas

First / Second / Third / Then / Next / Finally ....
The first / second / third / final point is ....

Third, having looked at customers and markets, the next issue is pricing.

Sequence ideas clearly.

Ending a section

Right / So / Well / OK ....
That's all I wanted to say about ....
I think that covers everything on ....
I think that deals with ....
To summarize,....

Intermediate questions

Are there any questions or comments on that?
Would anyone like to ask a question at this point?

I think that covers everything about our no smoking policy. Are there any questions on that?

Close points clearly and encourage questions!

Opening a new section

Let's now look at ....
Now I want to turn to ....
This brings me to the third and final point which is ....

Exploring a list of points

In relation to ....
Regarding ....
Concerning ....
With respect to ....

Another factor in our decision to relocate to Australia was the weather.

Add ideas to develop your argument.

Adding ideas

In addition to this .... / Moreover ....
However .... / Despite this ....
So .... / Therefore ....

Digressing

If I could just digress for a second, ...
I would like to look at ... in passing.
By the way .... / Incidentally ....

If I could just digress again for a second...

Going back

Let me now return to ....
Let me now come back to ....

Respect your audience.

Presentation tips
Signaling will:
- clarify the structure of your talk
- help the audience to understand what you are saying
- help to organize your thoughts as you give the presentation

D I A L O G http://access.englishcentral.com/compass/signalinglinkingparts

Fill in the blanks. Listen and check.

| come back to | ideas | deal with | questions |

Mark: ... It is important for customers to feel like their _____ are valued. I think that covers everything on my second point. Are there any _____ or comments at this point?

Bob: I have a question, Mark. What kind of system do you use for organizing and sharing this kind of customer feedback?

Mark: That's a great question. I plan to cover that a little later. I have some thoughts on ways to _____ sharing such feedback. I'll go over the final section of my presentation, then _____ your question. OK?

Bob: That's fine.

Mark: Now I want to return to how informal feedback can be encouraged ...

V O C A B U L A R Y

Match the phrases with similar meanings.

1. In relation to ...

2. Next I'd like to turn to ...

3. Now, to return to my point about ...

4. That's all I wanted to say about ...

5. To digress for moment ...

a. Coming back to what I was saying ...

b. I think that covers ...

c. Incidentally, let me tell you about ...

d. This brings me to my second point ...

e. With respect to ...

P R A C T I C E

Choose the best word to complete the sentence.

1. I don't think the ideas supported his _____ very well.

   a. argument   b. audience   c. factor   d. sequence

2. She used excellent visual aids to _____ the complex ideas for her audience.

   a. clarify   b. digress   c. question   d. signal

3. Half of the _____ got up and left during the middle of the presentation.

   a. audience   b. ideas   c. points   d. thoughts

4. If you do not _____ your points correctly, your presentation will not be effective.

   a. concern   b. digress   c. return   d. sequence

5. We had a hard time following the presentation because she did not _____ where one part of the presentation ended and the next began.

   a. deal with   b. return to   c. signal   d. turn to

4. Highlighting and emphasizing

Vocabulary

NOUNS
articulation
contrast
disaster
improvement
key word
option
repetition
solution
team work

VERBS
achieve
emphasize
highlight
reiterate
simplify
stress

ADJECTIVES
absolute
brilliant
complex
critical
dramatic
essential
important
outstanding
remarkable
simple

ADVERBS
basically
carefully
closely
exactly
frankly
repeatedly
simply
totally

Focusing

I'd like to emphasize ....
I'd like to stress ....
I should reiterate/repeat ....
It is critical/essential to understand ....

'What'

What we can't do is ....
What I'd like to do is ....
What we have been able to do is ....
What is really important is ....

Repetition

This is a **very**, **very** difficult problem.
We thought for a **long**, **long** time about this.
We **need** to do something and we **need** to do it now.

Simplifying

To be honest,..../Frankly speaking,....
Basically,..../To put it simply,....
Believe me,....

Analyzing

Let's look at this more closely.
What does this mean exactly?
In other words,....

Articulation – stressing

Auxiliary verbs – do / does / did
We **did** achieve many things last year.
It **does** seem to be the best solution.
We **did** think very carefully about this.

Key words
I agree, it **is** important.
We have tried **repeatedly**, believe me.
There is a **lot** of room for improvement.

Dramatic language

A total/absolute/complete disaster
A great/outstanding/remarkable success
Totally unacceptable/Quite brilliant

Contrast

Actually ..../In fact ..../In reality ..../The truth is that ....
Yesterday it was easy. **Today** it is far more difficult.

I'd like to emphasize the importance of team work.

This is a very, very complex problem.

Repeat in order to highlight.

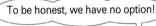
To be honest, we have no option!

Focus with simple phrases.

My first idea didn't work. But this idea can't fail, believe me!

Use dramatic contrast.

Little words:
Big impact

It is **so** simple.
It is **really** easy.
It is **far too** difficult.
It is **simply** brilliant.
It is **no** problem.

D I A L O G http://access.englishcentral.com/compass/highlightingemphasizing

Fill in the blanks. Listen and check.

Frankly	remarkable	reiterate	essential

Mark: We can contrast the results from the company's formal product feedback with the results I found in informal conversations. There is a _____ difference in both the type and quality of feedback from these two methods.

Linda: Do you think it's possible for anyone to achieve this kind of result through informal customer feedback?

Mark: _____ speaking, yes. Informal feedback is really simple to get. There is nothing complex about the method. The _____ point is that you have to create a space for it during meetings or conversations with clients.

Bob: The feedback is certainly an improvement over the formal feedback.

Mark: Exactly! Let me _____ it's critical to be open to hearing client feedback.

V O C A B U L A R Y

Write the adverbs with the verbs to create the given meaning.

basically	carefully	exactly	repeatedly	totally

VERBS	**ADVERBS**	
1. accept	_____	- agree about everything
2. consider	_____	- think deeply about
3. emphasize	_____	- say over and over
4. match	_____	- have all points the same
5. outline	_____	- explain in general terms

P R A C T I C E

Correct the error in each of the following sentences.

1. Our manager is constantly reminding us of the importance of team works.

2. The project turned into an absolutely disaster.

3. The solution he suggested is too far difficult.

4. To put it simple, this problem is only going to get worse if we don't act now.

5. We have seen a dramatical increase in complaints over the past year.

5. Engaging your audience

NOUNS
a show of hands
clarification
diplomacy
expectation
facts
neighbor
point of view
rapport
specialist
statistics

VERBS
acknowledge
afford
downsize
ignore
lead to
offer
spend time on
tend to

ADJECTIVES
diplomatic
recent
rhetorical
satisfied

Rhetorical questions

Are we satisfied with this product?
Do we really want to downsize?
Is this company growing fast enough?
Can we afford to ignore this problem?

Offer clarification

Is that clear?
Are there any questions about that?
I'm sure some of you want to take me up on this.

Directing questions

George, I know you have a lot of experience.
　　Could you comment?
Perhaps, I can ask Peter to answer that question? Peter?
I'd like to try an experiment.
　　Could you ask your neighbor ...?
Can I ask for a show of hands?
　　How many people ...?
How many people here have ever ...?

Creating rapport

We need to ....
We don't need to spend time on this.
I know what you are thinking.
I'm sure everyone in this room ....

Interesting facts

Did you know that ...?
According to a recent study ....
I read somewhere that ....
Statistics show that ....

Interesting examples

For example ....
For instance ....
As an example ....

Acknowledge

I'm sure you don't need me to tell you that ....
I realize you all know ....

Diplomacy – softening

I tend to think that ....
It seems to me that ....
It may be a little/bit difficult.

Is money really the greatest motivator?

Rhetorical questions create variety and expectation, leading to an interested audience!

Are there any questions?

Involve your audience by asking questions!

Did you know that 10% of the U.S. population is vegetarian?

ASSOCIATION　PROFESSIONAL BUTCHERS

Interest your audience with statistics.

This is what we call a mobile phone.

Anyone can see that ...

Be diplomatic/
Use diplomacy.

The audience are specialists too!

Quick tips
Build a rapport with your audience:
- Use "we" not "I."
- Understand their point of view.

D I A L O G   http://access.englishcentral.com/compass/engagingyouraudience

Fill in the blanks. Listen and check.

show of hands	diplomatic	point of view	acknowledge

Mark: Rapport with the client is critical.

Linda: In your _____, Mark, has informal feedback lead to any significant changes in the way you deal with clients?

Mark: I think it has made me more _____ in dealing with complaints.

Bob: I'd like to ask for clarification of what you mean by that.

Mark: Let me get a _____ of the number of people here who have lost their temper dealing with complaints? Lots of us. I tended to do that too. That was because my expectation was that I had to defend the product. Now I _____ the complaint as a situation where the client is offering informal feedback. Can we afford to ignore informal feedback from our clients?

V O C A B U L A R Y

What should a person ask in each case? Fill in the blanks.

for a show of hands	a rhetorical question	for clarification
to spend more time	to see statistics	

1. To continue a topic without going to the next topic, ask _____.
2. To count the number of people who agree, ask _____.
3. To get more information to understand better, ask _____.
4. To get people to think but not speak, ask _____.
5. To see proof according to numbers or research, ask _____.

P R A C T I C E

Choose the word with a similar meaning as the underlined word.

1. According to our most <u>current</u> research, customers prefer red to blue.
      a. diplomatic   b. recent   c. rhetorical   d. satisfied

2. I asked him to speak to us today because he is an <u>expert</u> in this field.
      a. clarification   b. expectation   c. fact   d. specialist

3. Please take a few minutes to discuss this problem with <u>the person next to you</u>.
      a. show of hands   b. your neighbor   c. point of view   d. rapport

4. As you can see from these <u>figures</u>, the market has greatly increased.
      a. facts   b. neighbors   c. specialists   d. statistics

5. You need to speak with more <u>politeness</u> so that you don't offend your audience.
      a. diplomacy   b. expectation   c. rapport   d. views

6. Visual aids – design and type

NOUNS
aspects
bar chart
color
curtain
diagram
first glance
flow chart
illustration
layout
map
marker
meaning
OHP
pie chart
plan
pointer
presenter
shape
slide
table
transparency
visual

VERBS
communicate
distract
draw attention to
illustrate

ADJECTIVES
compatible
logical
shaded
technical

Introducing the visual

OK. Let's take a look at ....
I have a transparency to show you.
The first/second/next/final slide is ....

Check with the audience

Is that clear for everyone?
Is that in focus?
Can everybody see that?

Meaning of the visual

This shows/illustrates/demonstrates/refers to ....
This is a graph/a diagram which shows ....
As you can see, this is ....
Here we can see ....

Focusing attention

I'd like to draw your attention to ....
One of the most important aspects of this is ....
At first glance it seems .... but ....

Type of visual

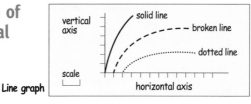

Line graph

Illustrate things
you can't say in words.

Why use a visual aid?

Saves time
Highlights key points
Creates impact
Helps the presenter
Creates variety
Builds interest

Spot check ---visuals

■ Are spelling and grammar correct?
■ Is lettering clear?
■ Is the layout logical?
■ Are the colors compatible?
■ Does it communicate or distract?

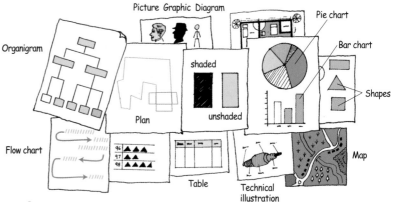

Equipment and environment

D I A L O G http://access.englishcentral.com/compass/visualaidsdesignandtype

Fill in the blanks. Listen and check.

color	illustrate	first glance	diagram

Mark: I have a transparency here to _____ how I organize informal feedback.
Bob: I think the OHP is out of focus. Can you fix it?
Mark: Sure. OK, that looks better. Where did the pointer go? Well, never mind. I can just use my hand. At _____, this system may look rather complicated. But it's actually very simple.
Linda: Do the different shapes mean types of files?
Mark: Actually, the shapes in the _____ represent organization within the file. And I would also like to draw your attention to the _____ coding of the shapes. The meaning of each color is related to the three situations I described before when informal feedback is given ...

V O C A B U L A R Y

Which visual aid is best to show the information? Write the choice in the blank.

bar chart	flow chart	diagram	pie chart	table

1. Use a _____ to show the growth in company expenses over the past five years.
2. Use a _____ to compare several features of three products to see similarities and differences.
3. Use a _____ to show the percent of customers (100%) who prefer different products.
4. Use a _____ to show the steps in the process of production for a product.
5. Use a _____ to show the relationship between various departments in an organization.

P R A C T I C E

Fill in the blanks in the following critique of a presentation's visual aids.

compatible	distracted	layout	technical

Presentation Critique

Visual Aids: 1. The colors of your slides and text are not _____. It was hard to read the yellow text on orange slides.
2. The _____ of your flow chart was very hard to follow. I couldn't understand it at all.
3. The animation on the slides _____ the audience from the information. We were all watching the moving animals.
4. There were many _____ problems during the presentation. Practice with the equipment before your presentation!

7. Visual aids – describing charts

NOUNS
deterioration
fluctuation
peak
recovery
slump

VERBS
deteriorate
fall
fluctuate
improve
reach a low point
recover
rocket
slump
worsen

ADJECTIVES
gradual
rapid
significant
slight
stable

ADVERBS
consequently
gradually
significantly
slightly

Describing change

Up
To go up
To increase — an increase
To rise — a rise
To grow — a growth
To improve — an improvement
To get better
To recover — a recovery
To rocket

up

rocket

Others
To remain stable
To level out
To reach a peak
To peak — a peak

peak

Down
To go down
To decrease — a decrease
To fall — a fall
To drop — a drop
To deteriorate — a deterioration
To get worse
To worsen — a worsening
To slump — a slump

down

slump

To fluctuate — a fluctuation
To bottom out
To reach a low point
To hit a low — a low

fluctuate

Speed of change
Rapid — Rapidly
Steady — Steadily
Gradual — Gradually
Slow — Slowly

Degree of change
Dramatic — Dramatically
Significant — Significantly
Moderate — Moderately
Slight — Slightly

Prepositions
To stand at
From .... to ....
By ....
An increase of ....

Sales rose rapidly.
There was a rapid rise in sales.

Sales rose dramatically.
There was a dramatic rise in sales.

7							
6							
5							
4							
3							
2							
1							
0		JAN 1999		JAN 2000			

Sales rose from 3 million to 7 million.
Sales rose by 4 million.
There was an increase of 4 million over last year.
Sales stood at 3 million in January.

Giving explanations

This was **a result of** bad planning.

The cause
This happened because ....
This was a result of ....
So ..../Therefore ....

The result
This will result in ....
This will lead to ....
Consequently ..../As a result ....

This will **lead to** job cuts.

D I A L O G   http://access.englishcentral.com/compass/visualaidsdescribingcharts

Fill in the blanks. Listen and check.

slump	deterioration	recovered	low point

Sam: The next slide we are going to look at shows the fluctuation of sales over the past two years.

Karen: Wow! Last quarter we hit quite a _____!

Sam: Yes, we did. And we can see in this graph that sales started to gradually worsen in the last quarter of the last year. They _____ slightly in the first quarter, but then continued to fall until the present quarter.

Mike: Any idea what caused this _____ in sales?

Sam: One significant factor is the economy. We're not the only ones facing this problem. But the good news is that I think we've achieved a _____, and things are going to improve in the next quarter.

V O C A B U L A R Y

Fill in the blanks using the correct word to complete the sentence.

decrease	fluctuate	improve	rocket	stable

1. A time over which there is no change is a time when sales are _____.

2. If sales drop, it means they _____.

3. Sales that go up and down several times over a short period _____.

4. Another way to say sales go up very fast is to say they _____.

5. When there is growth in the market, sales _____.

P R A C T I C E

Label the following parts shown on the graph.

fall	fluctuation	peak	recovery	rise

1. _____

2. _____

5. _____

4. _____

3. _____

8. Body language – being persuasive

Vocabulary

NOUNS
advantage
appearance
chaos
disadvantage
expression
gesture
posture
proposal
riot
stance
suicide

VERBS
convince
maintain
smile
take a break

ADJECTIVES
absolute
enormous
enthusiastic
facial
risky
stark
superior

Checklist
Match your appearance to audience expectations
Maintain eye contact
Use positive facial expressions --- smile
Move to create interest
Use hands to create impact with gesture
Establish a confident posture and stance
Create a positive attitude --- be relaxed and enthusiastic

Dress for your audience.

Relax.

Persuading language

Is that clear?

Proposing
I suggest that we ....
  My suggestion is that we ....
I recommend that we ....
  My recommendation is that we ....
I propose that we ....
  My proposal is that we ....

Smile

I suggest that we take a break.

Advantages
The difference between ... and ... is enormous.
What are the advantages and disadvantages of ...?
On the one hand .... / On the other hand ....
This is far superior to .... / better than ....

Stark options
We have no choice.
If we don't .... then we will see ....
Either we .... or ....
Instead of .... we could ....

Let's look at the advantages.

Neutral vs emotive words

Neutral	*Emotive*
It is **risky**.	It is commercial **suicide**.
This may be a **problem**.	This will lead to **chaos**.
We **require** this.	This is an **absolute must**.
Some will **complain**.	There will be a **riot**.

Marketing this product would be commercial suicide.

Say it three times!
          [1]   [2]   [3]
This new product is **faster**, **cheaper**, and **more efficient**.
This supplier is **friendly**, **customer-focused**, and **next door**!
      [1]   [2]   [3]

Persuade with emotive language.

Presentation tip
Practice the introduction until it is perfect.
You need to convince your audience in the first sixty seconds!

D I A L O G http://access.englishcentral.com/compass/bodylanguagebeingpersuasive

Fill in the blanks. Listen and check.

| proposal | posture | enthusiastic | facial |

Mike: Let's take a break before we discuss Sam's ideas further.
Karen: You gave a very interesting _____, Sam.
Sam: Thanks, Karen. I think this new approach has a lot of advantages.
Karen: I could tell through the presentation you're very _____ about it.
Sam: I just hope I convinced the managers. It's a little risky, you know.
Karen: Well, your _____ and stance during the presentation communicated your absolute confidence in the proposal.
Sam: What about my _____ expression when Mike wanted me to go over the statistics again?
Karen: You kept smiling. That was a good thing!

V O C A B U L A R Y

Match the words with similar meanings.

1. appearance   **a.** emotion

2. attitude   **b.** idea

3. gesture   **c.** looks

4. proposal   **d.** movement

5. stance   **e.** posture

P R A C T I C E

Choose the best word to complete the sentence.

1. He tried to _____ a positive attitude even though everything was going wrong.
   a. convince   b. maintain   c. smile   d. take

2. If you said those terrible things to the boss, it would be _____ for your career!
   a. advantage   b. gesture   c. riot   d. suicide

3. The company had to lay off hundreds of workers due to its _____ financial problems.
   a. absolute   b. enormous   c. facial   d. superior

4. There are few benefits with the change but many _____.
   a. appearance   b. chaos   c. disadvantages   d. stance

5. The new model is by far _____ to the old model.
   a. enormous   b. risky   c. stark   d. superior

9. Communicating styles

NOUNS
approach
catastrophe
competence
performance
strength
style
weakness

VERBS
balance
concentrate
exaggerate
overstate
perceive
translate
utilize

ADJECTIVES
balanced
detached
emphatic
impersonal
in-depth
organic
systematic

People have different communicating styles. Understanding how **you** communicate is important to improve your presentation planning and performance. Consider your own style by asking yourself the questions in the table below. Remember — there is no right or wrong way but you should have a balanced approach.

Communication factor	Personal profile
Systematic vs Organic	Do you prefer structured presentations to a more organic style?
Formal vs Informal	Do you prefer formal language, dress, posture to an informal approach?
Closed vs Open	Do you state facts or ask questions and discuss answers?
Complex vs Simple	Do you enjoy in-depth analysis or communicating simply and efficiently?
Emphatic vs Relaxed	Do you tend to overstate and exaggerate or just concentrate on the facts?
Involved vs Impersonal	Do you engage emotionally with your presentation subject or remain detached?

Language choices

Now examine some of the ways in which differences in communicating style translate into differences in the language which we use.

1. Choose between formality and informality

Formal Phrases		*Informal Phrases*
Good morning ladies and gentlemen	vs	Hello, everyone ....
On behalf of ... may I welcome you to	vs	Thanks for coming.
If I may, I'd now like to move on to	vs	OK. Secondly,....
If you have any questions, feel free	vs	Just interrupt with questions.

Formal Vocabulary		*Informal Vocabulary*
Sales have recovered.	vs	Sales have picked up.
We will acquire the company soon.	vs	We will buy it soon.
We perceive it differently.	vs	We see it differently.
We must utilize our competence.	vs	We must use our competence.

2. Balance personal against impersonal

Tense	*Passive - Impersonal*	*Active - Personal*
Present simple	It is thought	I think
Present continuous	It is being examined	We are examining
Present perfect	It has been claimed	An expert has claimed
Past simple	It was arranged	I arranged it.
Future	This will be looked at later.	I will look at this later.

3. Balance 'stating' against 'questioning'

It is clear that	vs	Would you agree that ...?
I don't think that	vs	Do you think that ...?
We must	vs	Is there any way to ...?

4. Balance 'emphatic' against 'relaxed'

This is a really big problem	vs	This is a slight worry
This is a catastrophe	vs	This may cause a problem
I am convinced	vs	I tend to think that ....

Presentation tip

Focus on your strengths.
Work on your weaknesses.

D I A L O G   http://access.englishcentral.com/compass/presentationscommunicatingstyles

Fill in the blanks. Listen and check.

utilize	balanced	exaggerating	in-depth

Sam: It would be a real catastrophe to continue business as usual.
Mike: I think you're _____ the danger a bit.
Sam: Without changing our approach, we'll never improve performance.
Karen: Sam is right. If we _____ the new approach in a systematic way, our sales should rocket by early next year.
Mike: We need to do more _____ research on this approach. We need to balance its strengths and weaknesses before we apply it. Sam's presentation concentrated too heavily on the benefits. I want to see the other side.
Karen: I disagree. I thought the presentation was well _____ regarding the positive and negative aspects of the approach.

V O C A B U L A R Y

Match each sentence with the kind of communication style it represents.

1. detached   a. I want to hear the ideas you have on this topic.

2. emphatic   b. These are the five points I'll cover in today's presentation.

3. open   c. If that happens, it will be a catastrophe for our company.

4. organic   d. We need to look at this problem logically.

5. systematic   e. I won't follow an outline. I'll let our discussion lead the
                                 flow of the presentation.

P R A C T I C E

Label the following sentences as either Formal or Informal.

1. Here at Word Corp., we see things a little differently. _____

2. Managers have not been utilizing the full potential of the competence of many of our senior employees. _____

3. On behalf of Star Enterprises, I want to welcome everyone to today's workshop. _____

4. The seriousness of the situation cannot be overstated. _____

5. Let me ask you all something: "Is this the how we want people to think of this company?"

_____

10. Closing a presentation

NOUNS
attention
handout
recommendation

VERBS
advise
conclude
expect
follow up
go over
invite
recommend
sum up
summarize

ADJECTIVES
final

ADVERBS
attentively
briefly

Signaling the end

OK. That brings me to the end of my presentation.
Right. That covers everything I wanted to say about ....
So, that's all I have to say.

That brings me to the end of my presentation.

Summarizing

To sum up then,....
In brief,....
Before I finish, let me just go over ....
If I can briefly summarize,....

Concluding

To conclude, I'd like to say that ....
I'd like to finish by saying ....
In conclusion,....

I'd like to finish by singing you a song.

Have a strong finish.

Final recommendation

It seems to me, then, that we should ....
I would therefore recommend / advise that ....

I've prepared a handout.

Support

I have prepared a handout which I will pass round.
I'll give you my e-mail address in case you want to follow
up on something I said.

Closing

Thank you for listening so attentively.
Thank you for your attention.
I hope that this has been useful.

Thank you for your attention.

Inviting questions

I'd be glad to answer any questions.
So, do you have any questions?
Are there any questions?
Yes, the gentleman / lady sitting there. [*points*]

Are there any questions?

Presentation tip
Prepare answers to questions which you expect.

D I A L O G http://access.englishcentral.com/compass/presentationsclosing

Fill in the blanks. Listen and check.

conclude	summarize	invite	attention

Mark: I want to briefly _____ the benefits of informal feedback. It can provide more detailed information about clients' needs, it makes clients feel empowered, and it strengthens the customer-client relationship. So, to _____, I would like to recommend that the sales department utilize informal feedback in a more systematic way in the future. Thank you for your _____. I expect many of you have questions, so I would now like to _____ your questions regarding my presentation.

V O C A B U L A R Y

Correct the mistake in each of the following sentences.

1. He adviced the employee to rewrite the proposal.

2. I want to go over to these statistics very carefully so everyone can see my point.

3. It is the strong recommend of the committee that the project be funded.

4. My finally point is that we need to give more attention to this area in the future.

5. She made hand outs of her slides to help the audience write notes during the presentation.

P R A C T I C E

Put the following sentences in order as a conclusion to a presentation. (a = first, e = last)

_____ 1. I'll be happy to answer any questions if there are any.

_____ 2. Thank you for listening so attentively to my presentation.

_____ 3. That was everything I wanted to say on how to review a plan.

_____ 4. Yes, Maggie? Do you have a question?

_____ 5. To go over the three recommendations one last time, we need to 1) plan our strategy, 2) implement our plan, and 3) follow up with a review of its effectiveness.

11. Handling questions

Vocabulary

NOUNS
area
criticism
field
response

VERBS
catch
depend on
follow
hedge
make clear
mention
point out
refer back
repeat

ADJECTIVES
complex
complicated
confidential
difficult
fair
glad
interesting
positive

ADVERBS
correctly

Questions for the presenter

> Are you saying that...?

> What did you mean when you said ...?

> Could you go over that again, please? It wasn't very clear for me.

> Could you say a little bit more about ...?

> Don't you think that ...?

Positive response

That's a good / difficult / complex / an interesting question.
Thank you for asking that question.
I'm glad someone asked that question. It allows me to say ....

> I wish you hadn't asked that.

> That's an interesting question.

Check your answer

Does that answer your question? / Is that OK?
Is that clear now? / Can we move on?

Clarify

If I understand you correctly, you want to know ....
You're asking me about .... Is that right?
Sorry I didn't follow / catch the question.
Could you repeat that for me, please?
In other words, you're asking ....

> What do you mean?

> If I understand you correctly, you're asking me about ....

> Didn't you listen?

Refer back

As I said earlier, in the first section / at the end of the second section ....
Yes, I mentioned in the introduction ....

Accept criticism

I accept that. / That's a fair point. / I agree with what you're saying.
Up to a point, I agree.

> As I said earlier, ...

Referring back to the presentation

As said / pointed out / explained earlier,....
I think we've already made it clear that ....

> I should have done more preparation.

Avoiding:

1. Wrong person

I'm afraid I can't really answer that.
That's not really my area / field, I'm afraid.
I don't have the figures with me.

> That's not really my field.

2. Wrong topic

I'm afraid that question goes beyond the subject of today's presentation.
I'm afraid that's confidential. / I'm not at liberty to give you that information.
I'd be glad to discuss that with you personally after the presentation.

3. Tennis – returning a question

Well, let me ask you the same question.
OK. Let me ask you a question.
I can answer that by asking you a question.

> I'd be fired if I told you that!

4. Hedging

Well, that depends on what you mean by ....
Well, it's a very complicated matter ....
Well, there are various ways of looking at it.

> I'm afraid that is confidential.

D I A L O G http://access.englishcentral.com/compass/presentationshandlingquestions

Fill in the blanks. Listen and check.

follow	hedging	difficult	depend on

Bob: If I understand you correctly, you mean the feedback led to larger orders.

Mark: Of course it is _____ to prove a real cause and effect relationship between the feedback and sales.

Bob: Now you sound like you're _____ on the claims you made before.

Mark: Let me make one thing clear. I am positive informal feedback led to a better relationship with clients. And I'll also mention that sales do not _____ the relationship alone, but a good relationship certainly doesn't hurt.

Linda: I have a question, too. I didn't _____ your organization of feedback files. Can you repeat that for me, please?

V O C A B U L A R Y

Match the question with the correct response.

1. Can we move on to the next question?   **a.** It's both fair and objective.

2. Did I understand you correctly?   **b.** It's a complex area to study.

3. Is that really a fair criticism of the project?   **c.** Yes, that's what I said.

4. Would you tell us more about who did the study?   **d.** No, I also want to point out...

5. How can you study the market response to this product?   **e.** I'm afraid I can't. That is confidential information.

P R A C T I C E

Choose the word with a similar meaning as the underlined word.

1. He could not give an <u>answer</u> to the question.

   a. area   b. criticism   c. field   d. response

2. I'll be <u>happy</u> to talk with you about that after the meeting.

   a. complicated   b. fair   c. glad   d. interesting

3. She <u>made reference</u> to an earlier point in her presentation.

   a. depended on   b. made clear   c. pointed out   d. referred back

4. We don't know much about current research in this <u>area</u>.

   a. criticism   b. field   c. response   d. section

5. I'm sorry. I didn't <u>hear</u> what you said.

   a. catch   b. hedge   c. mention   d. repeat

12. Presenting at a glance

Vocabulary

NOUNS
body
ending
greeting
introduction
length

VERBS
close
digress
greet
handle
highlight
introduce
open
outline
sequence
signal
state

ADJECTIVES
positively

Introduction

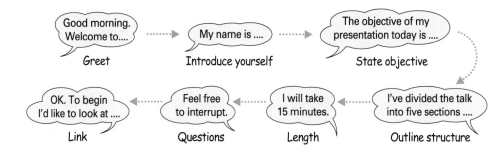

Main Body

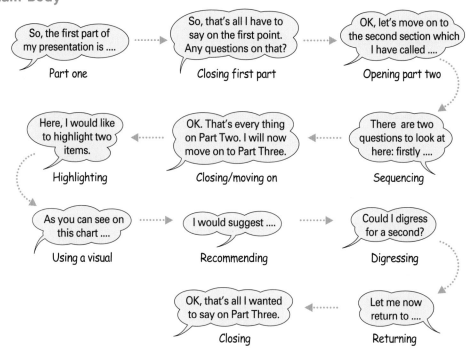

Ending

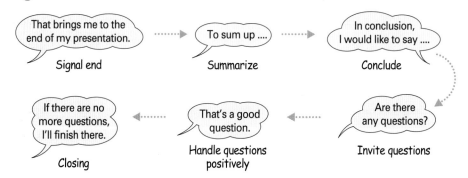

Fill in the blanks. Listen and check.

body	greeting	digress	handled

Mark: So what did you think of the presentation, Linda?

Linda: I think the way you introduced yourself in the _____ really helped break the ice in the meeting.

Mark: I wanted everyone to feel relaxed.

Linda: And in the _____ of the presentation, you outlined your points very well. You stated the information clearly and didn't _____ from the topic.

Mark: What did you think about the length of the presentation?

Linda: It was good. When you closed, I thought you _____ all the questions from the audience well.

Mark: Thanks for your feedback, Linda.

VOCABULARY

In which part of a presentation should you do each thing? Write the part in the blank.

Introduction	Body	Ending

1. refer to a chart _____

2. greet the audience _____

3. invite people to ask questions _____

4. state your objective _____

5. summarize your main points _____

PRACTICE

Match the sentences with similar meanings.

1. Allow me to digress for just a few minutes.

2. Feel free to interrupt.

3. Looking now at my second topic ...

4. That's a good question.

5. I'd like to welcome everyone to today's presentation.

a. Good afternoon.

b. I'm glad you asked me that.

c. Let's move on to my next point.

d. That reminds me of a story.

e. I'll be happy to answer questions at any time.

13. Cross-cultural tips

Vocabulary

NOUNS
analysis
animation
dress code
factor
hierarchy
host
hostility
interaction
interruption
lack
organization
personality
pocket
precision
professionalism
punctuality
role
sloppiness
spontaneity

VERBS
bear with
consider
contribute
interrupt

ADJECTIVES
dynamic
irrelevant
reserved
rigid
specific
strict
sufficient
suitable

Remember....

Audiences have very different expectations in different cultures. Knowing what your audience expects from the presenter is critical to successful presenting. When preparing and planning presentations for specific audiences, you should consider the following:

Involvement Factor

Interaction:	Some audiences simply want to listen and not contribute.
Role of silence:	Some audiences use silence to communicate agreement, not hostility.
Interruption:	Some audiences expect to be able to interrupt.
Human touch:	Some audiences like to see the personality of the presenter.
Punctuality:	Most audiences respect punctuality.
Formality:	Some audiences see informality as a lack of professionalism.
Animation:	Some audiences prefer a reserved style to over-enthusiastic presenters.
Level of analysis:	Many audiences have in-depth specialist knowledge.

Organization Factor

Systematic:	Some audiences prefer an organic style to rigid structure.
Support:	Some audiences don't want a lot of visuals and handouts.
Digression:	Some audiences see digression as irrelevant.

Body Language Factor

Hands:	Some audiences view hand(s) in pockets as sloppiness.
Eye contact:	Some audiences feel uncomfortable without eye contact.
Dress:	Some audiences work in companies and cultures with strict dress codes.
Body:	Some audiences expect a presenter to be dynamic.
Face:	Some audiences look for animated facial expressions.

Delivery Factor

Language:	Some audiences have a limited English vocabulary.
Reading text:	Some audiences favor spontaneity over precision.
Voice:	ALL audiences need sufficient volume and a suitable speed.

Social Factor

Names:	Some audiences prefer family names to first names.
Business card:	Some audiences will request a business card.
Host thanking:	ALL audiences expect basic courtesies. Be polite.
Hierarchy:	ALL audiences respect social and corporate hierarchies.

Survival strategies

Situation	Language
The audience doesn't understand.	Let me go over that again.
You forgot!	Perhaps I should mention ....
No vocabulary!	I'm sorry, what's that word again?
You are lost.	Now, where was I?
You drop your slides!	Please, just bear with me a second.
No time.	So, the main point is ....

D I A L O G http://access.englishcentral.com/compass/presentationscrossculturaltips

Fill in the blanks. Listen and check.

specific	interrupt	bear with me	contribute

Bob: Have you considered giving a workshop on presentations, Mark?

Mark: What are you talking about, Bob? You must be kidding.

Bob: No, _____ for a minute. I thought you gave a very dynamic presentation.

Mark: Really? I sensed a bit of hostility during the questions at the end.

Bob: Not at all. I just wanted you to be _____ about the value you see in . . .

Mark: Of course I never did any formal analysis of the benefits of informal feedback.

Bob: Don't _____. I was trying to tell you the organization, interaction, and professionalism of your presentation were impressive. Maybe you could _____ some tips to help others here give better presentations.

V O C A B U L A R Y

Find an adjective in the Vocabulary list with a similar meaning. Write the word.

1. appropriate   _____

2. energetic   _____

3. enough   _____

4. not important   _____

5. stiff   _____

P R A C T I C E

Write the correct word in the blank to complete the definition.

dress code	hierarchy	lack	punctuality	spontaneity

1. A _____ lists rules for what you can or can't wear at work.

2. If a person can improvise well, she or he has _____.

3. A _____ refers to the different levels of power in a society or organization.

4. If there is a _____ of something, that thing is not enough or does not exist.

5. A person with _____ is always on time.

14. Golden rules

Practice and rehearse key English phrases.

NOUNS
anecdote
assumption
clarity
facilities
impact
intonation
joke
location
mannerism
overhead
preparation
spontaneity
text
view
volume

VERBS
block
establish
photocopy
practice

ADJECTIVES
cultural
distracting
inappropriate
scripted
sufficient

ADVERBS
positively
professionally

DO
- establish a clear objective.
- talk about what your audience expect you to talk about.
- organize the information.
- use notes or key words to assist.
- have a strong opening and closing.
- make it interesting.
- use your voice for effect.
- keep it simple.
- use visuals which improve impact and clarity.
- handle equipment professionally.
- speak with sufficient volume and intonation.
- use summaries to link the parts.
- think about the cultural environment.
- dress for the occasion.
- prepare and practice beforehand.
- be confident and relaxed.
- balance spontaneity and preparation.
- handle questions positively.

Use visuals which improve
impact and clarity.

DON'T
- make assumptions about the location and facilities –check beforehand.
- present information which is too complex for the audience.
- talk for too long.
- tell irrelevant anecdotes or inappropriate jokes.
- speak too quickly.
- use too many visuals.
- photocopy small text onto an overhead.
- read from a scripted text or visuals.
- block your audience's view of a visual.
- talk with your back to the audience.
- use distracting mannerisms.
- forget to summarize at the end.

Don't block your audience's view.

D I A L O G http://access.englishcentral.com/compass/goldenrulesinpresenting

Fill in the blanks. Listen and check.

distracting	anecdotes	spontaneity	appropriate

Mark: So those are the best tips I can give you on how to give a presentation. Any questions?

Linda: How can we figure out if we have _____ mannerisms or not?

Mark: You have to practice in front of a mirror watching yourself speak.

Jeff: What about telling jokes or _____ during a presentation? Is that OK?

Mark: Positive jokes are _____ for presentations. A good anecdote could be helpful for explaining your point in a presentation. So if it helps the clarity of your point, I think an anecdote is fine.

Nancy: Do you prefer scripted presentations or do you leave room for _____?

Mark: Usually the text from my slides is enough. I don't write everything.

V O C A B U L A R Y

Mark each idea as good (DO) or bad (DON'T) according to the Golden Rules.

	DO	DON'T
1. Speak loudly during the presentation.	( )	( )
2. Tell lots of jokes to keep your audience laughing.	( )	( )
3. Use small letters to get more information on an overhead.	( )	( )
4. Explain the point you hope to make in the introduction.	( )	( )
5. Write everything down so you can just read it during the presentation.	( )	( )

P R A C T I C E

Use the words to complete the evaluation of the presentation.

blocked	established	preparation	sufficient	volume

Good points:

1. The objective of the presentation was clearly _____ in the intro.

2. You gave us _____ background to understand the problem.

3. Great _____! I could tell you practiced a lot.

Bad points:

1. You stood in the way and _____ our view of the flip chart.

2. You did not speak with enough _____. I couldn't hear you.

CHAPTER 3

English for Meetings

1. What makes a good meeting?
2. Meetings: key terms
3. Opening a meeting
4. Giving and responding to opinions
5. Controlling
6. Interruptions
7. Asking questions
8. Making decisions
9. Closing a meeting
10. Problem-solving meetings
11. Vocabulary building
12. Meetings at a glance
13. Cross-cultural tips
14. Golden rules

1. What makes a good meeting?

Preparation – a checklist

Successful meetings require good planning. The following is a checklist of essential planning items to consider:

Time and place	When and where is the meeting? Length — how long will it last?
People	Who will attend? Who will chair?
Roles	Do participants have special responsibilities? Will people have time to prepare input?
Purpose	What is the objective of the meeting? What is the agenda?
Type of meeting	Purpose of meeting: briefing? brainstorming?
Facilities	Do we have a room with equipment? What about refreshments, car parking, etc?
Communication	What documentation is required? Who will prepare and circulate it?

Execution – a checklist

Meetings consist of a chairperson and participants. Both have specific responsibilities to guarantee that a meeting is effective. A combination of language and general communication skills is essential.

Effective chairing

Opens ➤ Welcomes ➤ Outlines agenda and objectives, states procedure and roles ➤ Agrees on length of meeting ➤ Invites opinions ➤ Checks and clarifies ➤ Creates positive atmosphere ➤ Limits digression ➤ Keeps on track ➤ Encourages people to speak ➤ Builds to decision ➤ Watches time ➤ Reaches objectives ➤ Summarizes ➤ Closes and thanks

Effective participating

Presents opinions ➤ Listens to others ➤ Proposes ideas, asks questions ➤ Works efficiently ➤ Takes turns ➤ Respects other views ➤ Concentrates ➤ Agrees ➤ Disagrees politely ➤ Builds to decisions ➤ Understands the result

D I A L O G http://access.englishcentral.com/compass/goodmeeting

Fill in the blanks. Listen and check.

propose	refreshments	attend	circulating

Linda: Did you see the memo that is _____ the office?
Mark: Do you mean the one about the meeting tomorrow? Yeah, I saw it.
Linda: I'm still not sure what the meeting is about.
Mark: We're supposed to brainstorm ideas for better sales approaches.
Linda: Is it essential that everyone _____ the meeting? I was planning to be out of the office tomorrow afternoon.
Mark: Of course it's important. Bob is going to chair the meeting. I think he is going to _____ an idea he came up with.
Linda: I guess the length of the meeting will be at least a few hours. I hope we have _____.

V O C A B U L A R Y

Match each word with people or things it includes.

1. documents
2. equipment
3. facilities
4. refreshments
5. roles

a. chair, secretary, participant
b. coffee, sandwiches, fruit
c. memos, handouts, minutes
d. overhead, microphone, VCR
e. conference room, tables, chairs

P R A C T I C E

Fill in the blanks in the following memo.

agenda	attend	combination	positive	propose

MEMO

TO: All staff
FROM: Don Jones
RE: Staff meeting

This is just to remind everyone about the _____ for Friday's meeting. The meeting will be a _____ briefing and brainstorming session. Please come prepared to _____ ideas for reorganizing the office! And remember that we want to maintain a _____ atmosphere in the meeting. We won't criticize any ideas you share. All staff members are expected to _____ the meeting!

2. Meetings: key terms

NOUNS
agenda
break
chair
issue
item
matters
participant
point
proposal
recommendations
secretary

VERBS
adjourn
arise
be scheduled for
close
draw up
kick off
nominate
open
resume
run through
take a break
take place
write up

The process

Before the meeting **takes place**, it is important to invite **participants** to propose **items** or **points** for the **agenda**. **Drawing up** the agenda is usually the responsibility of the **secretary** or the **chair**. When the chair **opens** the meeting, it is usual to **run through** the agenda quickly. The first **item** is usually **Matters Arising**, to allow participants to go through the **minutes** of the previous meeting. After this, the discussion of the other **points** can begin. During the discussion, participants make **recommendations** and **proposals** in order to **solve** problems. If the meeting **is scheduled** for a whole day, it is typical to **take breaks** and **to adjourn** for lunch. Of course, it is necessary **to resume** [start again] after lunch. In the middle of the afternoon, participants often ask for **a time out** if they are feeling tired. At the end of the meeting, the last or next-to-last point is often **AOB** (Any Other Business) which gives participants the opportunity to **raise** other **issues** not included in the main agenda. During the meeting someone is **nominated** to **take** the minutes and after the meeting this person will **write up** the minutes for **circulation** to the other participants before the next meeting. Finally, the chair will **close** the meeting.

> **Note**
> A chair = chairperson -- chairman -- chairwoman
> To chair a meeting

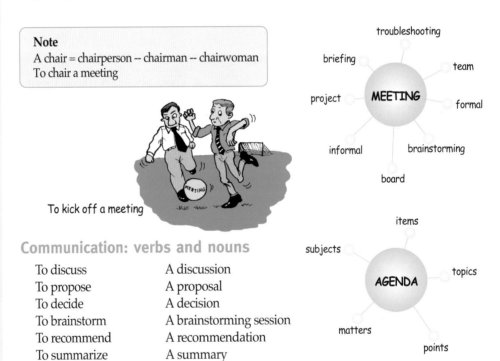

To kick off a meeting

Communication: verbs and nouns

To discuss   A discussion
To propose   A proposal
To decide   A decision
To brainstorm   A brainstorming session
To recommend   A recommendation
To summarize   A summary

Arrangements:

verbs + a 'meeting'

To organize
To schedule
To rearrange
To reschedule
To cancel

Arranging a meeting
A: Can we schedule a meeting to discuss the budget?
B: Of course.

A: Can you make it on Tuesday next week?
B: Yes, I can make Tuesday.

A: Shall we say 2 o'clock?
B: That would be fine.

A: We can hold the meeting in Room 26.
B: OK. Great.

A: I'll confirm this by e-mail.
B: OK, see you on Tuesday at 2.

A: I look forward to it.

D I A L O G http://access.englishcentral.com/compass/meetingskeyterms

Fill in the blanks. Listen and check.

adjourns	nominate	recommendations	writes up

Linda: Do you know if any other items are on the agenda for tomorrow's meeting?

Mark: All I know is that the chair will share his _____ for new sales techniques and then he'll ask all the participants to share their ideas.

Linda: Did the chair already _____ someone to be secretary for the meeting?

Mark: I don't think so. Usually Karen _____ the minutes of meetings in our department. She's always the unofficial secretary.

Linda: What time is the meeting going to take place?

Mark: It's scheduled for 2:30 in the conference room.

Linda: I hope it _____ before 5:00.

Mark: As long as no major issues arise, it'll probably finish by then.

P R A C T I C E

Write the word to complete the sentence.

break	kick off	matters	point	proposal

1. A short time to relax is also called a _____.

2. If you make a suggestion, it could be in the form of a _____.

3. The key idea is also the main _____.

4. Another term for issues or important subjects is _____.

5. To "_____" a meeting means the same as to start it.

V O C A B U L A R Y

Put the following meeting process in order (a=first, e=last).

_____ **1.** Allow participants to take a break.

_____ **2.** Close the meeting.

_____ **3.** Draw up the agenda for the meeting.

_____ **4.** Resume the meeting.

_____ **5.** Run through the minutes of the previous meeting.

3. Opening a meeting

Starting

Let's get down to business.
OK, shall we make a start?
Right, let's begin.

Welcoming and introducing

Welcome, everybody.
I'd like to start by welcoming everybody.
Firstly, I'd like to introduce ....
I don't think everyone knows ....

Apologies for absence

I'm afraid that ... cannot be with us today because ....
I have received apologies for absence from ....

Defining the objective

Our objective today is to ....
I've called this meeting to look at the question of ....
By the end of this meeting we should have ....

Introducing the agenda

Have you all seen a copy of the agenda?
OK. As you can see from the agenda, there are ... items.
Firstly ..., secondly ..., thirdly ..., finally ....
I suggest we follow the agenda.
Can we start with ... then go on to, ... and finish with ...?
Is there any other business?

The minutes

John will be taking the minutes.
Tim, could you take the minutes?

Process and roles

I suggest we go around the table first.
I'd like to hear what everyone thinks before we make a decision.
Firstly, I would like to give you a little more background.
Perhaps I should start by outlining my view on this.
Mr. Gonzales is going to take us through point one.

Length of meeting

I would like to finish by three o'clock.
The meeting is scheduled to finish at ....
We're short of time, so can I ask you to be brief?
Can we keep each item to fifteen minutes?

Let's begin

So, the first item on the agenda is ....
Right, let's start with ....
Mr. Chin, could you introduce this item?
Abu Bakar, would you like to start with the first point?

Checklist:
Opening
- Welcome
- Introduce, if necessary
- Apologies for absence
- Define the objective
- Introduce the agenda
- Confirm the minute-taker
- Explain the procedure
- Allocate roles
- Agree on length

Our target today is...

Define the objective

The computer will be taking the minutes.

I would like to finish by four o'clock.

DIALOG http://access.englishcentral.com/compass/meetingsopening

Fill in the blanks. Listen and check.

take minutes	go around	target	absence

Bob: OK. Let's get down to business. First, I'd like to welcome everybody to today's meeting. Jeff sends his apologies for his _____ from today's meeting. His son is sick. The objective of our meeting today is to brainstorm ideas for more effective sales techniques. That is our _____ this afternoon. I have a few ideas I'd like to share first, and then we will _____ the table and hear other ideas from each person here today. We'll try to keep to ten minutes for the discussion of each idea. That way the meeting won't run too long. And I've asked Karen to _____ for the meeting. So, as background I'd just like to take you through the standard sales techniques used in our department ...

VOCABULARY

Match the verb with the correct object.

VERBS	OBJECTS
1. allocate	**a.** main points
2. go around	**b.** business
3. outline	**c.** funds
4. take	**d.** minutes
5. get down to	**e.** the table

PRACTICE

Correct the mistake in each of the following sentences.

1. He wanted to keep the meeting through less than one hour.

2. I'd like to start by giving you some backgrounds about the project.

3. She located each person a special role at the meeting.

4. Tom will be our minute-person at this meeting.

5. Wendy sends her apologizes because she couldn't come to the meeting today.

4. Giving and responding to opinions

Vocabulary

NOUNS
case
efficiency
extent
opinions
thoughts
view

VERBS
be in favor of
comment
focus
hear from
respond
support
understate

ADJECTIVES
direct
negative
right

ADVERBS
absolutely
negatively
positively
totally

Asking for opinions	Involving people
What do you think?	We haven't heard from you yet, Bob.
What are your thoughts about this?	Can we hear what Jeremy has to say?
What is your opinion about this?	Susan, you're very quiet. Would you like to comment?
Recommending	**Comments to support and focus**
I think we should	That's a great idea! (*responding positively*)
Why don't we ...?	Yes, that might work. (*supporting*)
Maybe we could	Possibly yes, but .... (*supporting and focusing*)
How about ...?	I'm not so sure about that. (*responding negatively*)

Do you agree?	Agreeing with someone	Agreeing to something
Agreement	I totally agree with you.	I can agree to that ....
	I completely agree.	I support that ....
	Absolutely.	I'm in favor of that.
Part agreement	I see what you're saying but	I can partly agree to that but ....
	To a certain extent I agree but	That may be right but ....
	You may be right but	I'm not totally convinced because ....
Disagreement	I totally disagree with you.	I'm afraid I can't agree to that.
	I don't agree.	I can't support that.
	I'm not sure.	I'm against that because ....

Disagreement – diplomatic language

1. **Would, could** and **may** are less direct: ·····➤ This is a problem.
This **could / would / may** be a problem.

2. Understate by adding: **a little, a bit** ·····➤ You are behind schedule.
You are **a little / a bit** behind schedule.

3. Avoid negative words: awful terrible ·····➤ It was awful / terrible.
Use **not very** + positive word This is **not very good**.

Expressing opinion – a scale

I'm convinced that .... I'm sure that	Strong expression
I feel that .... In my opinion .... My view is that.... As I see it .... It seems to me	Neutral expression
I tend to think that .... I would suggest that .... It might be the case that	Weak expression

In my opinion...

It would ....
- save money.
- improve efficiency.
- reduce costs.

It wouldn't ....
- work.
- be easy.
- cost a lot of money.

D I A L O G http://access.englishcentral.com/compass/meetingsgivingandrespondingtoopinions

Fill in the blanks. Listen and check.

hear from	comment	extent	negatively

Bob: Would anyone like to _____ on that last suggestion?

Linda: I totally agree with you, Bob. I can see how it could really help sales.

Karen: I think to a certain _____ it might work, but perhaps not in the case of every client. Sometimes clients appreciate a more direct approach.

Mark: Karen is right. I can think of a few cases when clients have reacted _____ to the approach you've outlined, Bob.

Bob: Of course I am in favor of using a range of techniques to suit different clients. Why don't we _____ other people at the table now. Who else has an idea to share with us?

V O C A B U L A R Y

Mark each sentence as either showing agreement or disagreement.

	Agree	Disagree
1. I absolutely am not in favor of that.	( )	( )
2. I'm not so sure about that.	( )	( )
3. I can't go along with you on that.	( )	( )
4. I'm totally on your side about that.	( )	( )
5. I support that opinion.	( )	( )

P R A C T I C E

Choose the best word to complete the sentence.

1. I would like to _____ to that last comment.

    a. hear   b. reduce   c. respond   d. understate

2. Many people have responded _____ to the new advertising campaign.

    a. absolutely   b. partly   c. positively   d. totally

3. Please share your _____ with the rest of us. We'd like to hear them.

    a. costs   b. extent   c. efficiency   d. thoughts

4. Several members of this group seem to hold a _____ view of this plan.

    a. direct   b. negative   c. quiet   d. very

5. We need to _____ on the key issue, not irrelevant details.

    a. agree   b. favor   c. focus   d. support

5. Controlling

Vocabulary

VERBS
mean
reformulate
motivate
clarify
get side-tracked
stick to
move on
deal with
skip
come to

ADJECTIVES
relevant
outside the scope of
clear

Active listening: responding to motivate

Right.
OK. Yes, I see.
Thank you.

Active listening: reformulating to clarify

In other words, ...
So you think that ....
You mean that ....

Moving off the point

Could I digress for a minute?
It's not on the agenda but ....

Keeping to the agenda

I think we are digressing. Can we come back to the main question?
I think we're getting side-tracked. The main question is ....
I'm not sure that is strictly relevant. Can we return to ....
That is outside the scope of this meeting. Can we stick to the agenda, please?

Referring forward

We'll come to that later.
We'll be dealing with that in a moment.
Can we get to that later?

Referring back

As we said earlier, ...
We have already discussed this.

Postponing

Shall we skip this item?
I think we can forget point four. We've already discussed it.
I suggest that we deal with this at another meeting.

Length of meeting

We're pretty short of time.
Can we move on?
That's fifteen minutes on this.
   We agreed ten minutes per item. Let's move on.

Confirming a decision

OK. So we have decided to ....
Does everyone agree with that?
Is that clear?

Closing and moving on

I think that's everything on that.
Can we leave this point now and move on to the next item?
The next item on the agenda is ....
Now we come to the question of ....

That's interesting.

Good idea. Thank you for that.

In other words...

Effective chairing means responding and reformulating to motivate and clarify.

We're running a little over time. Can we move on?

Does everyone agree with that?

PAY RAISE
Chairman - 20%
Executives - 5%

Confirm and clarify decisions

DIALOG http://access.englishcentral.com/compass/meetingscontrolling

Fill in the blanks. Listen and check.

| reformulate | side-tracked | move on | scope |

Mark: There is no easy way to deal with overdue accounts.

Linda: We should set up a committee to _____ our accounting procedures.

Karen: I've often had to clarify our company's policy on payment options for clients. Some of the procedures are not very clear in company documents.

Bob: I think we're getting _____. We should stick to our original topic of discussion. Accounting and client payments are outside the _____ of this discussion. Let's focus our discussion on sales techniques. Maybe we should _____ to the next person's ideas. I believe Linda was next ...

VOCABULARY

Match the sentences with similar meanings.

1. I don't think that is really relevant.
2. Let's skip that question for now.
3. I hope that is clear for everyone.
4. We're getting side-tracked.
5. I'm not sure what you mean.

a. I assume all of you understand it.
b. I don't want to talk about it at this time.
c. I need you to clarify that for me.
d. It's not important.
e. The focus of the meeting is being lost.

PRACTICE

Fill in the blanks with the correct word.

| clarify | come to | motivate | reformulate | skip |

1. He tried to _____ people to come to the meetings by serving fancy refreshments.

2. If you don't _____ the meeting, the manager will notice your absence.

3. Obviously our original plan isn't working, so we need to _____ it to get this company back on track.

4. She just confused everybody more by giving all those statistics to try and _____ her point.

5. Since time is short, let's _____ these last two points and discuss recommendations.

6. Interruptions

Vocabulary

VERBS
add
come back to
come in
develop
exploit
interrupt
make a point
mention
point out

ADJECTIVES
relevant
worth

ADVERBS
at once
in more depth
namely
superficially

Chair – interrupting

OK. John, if I could just interrupt you there ....
Mary, sorry but I'd like to hear some other views on this.
OK. Thank you, Bob. You've made your point.

Chair – stopping an interruption

Just a moment, Peter. I'll come back to you when Mary has finished.
We can't all speak at once. One at a time, please. Peter, you wanted to ...?
Please, let him finish.

Participants – interrupting

Excuse me, may I interrupt?
Can I come in here?
Could I just comment on that?

Participants – stopping an interruption

If I could just finish.
May I just finish?
No, just one minute ....
I haven't finished what I was saying.

Why did you interrupt?

I'd like to point out ....
I'd like to add something to ....
I think we are forgetting an important point: namely ....
I'd like to develop one point that was mentioned by ....

Referring to other opinions

Peter, you said that ....
Somebody mentioned ....
What you said about ....
As Peter suggested,....

Changing the focus of the discussion

We need to go into this in more depth / detail.
We're looking at this too superficially.
There is another way of looking at this.
Perhaps ... is worth considering.

Commenting on an interruption

That's a good point.
I see what you mean.
You're right.

Chair – exploiting an interruption

OK. Perhaps we should talk more about ....
So, is it perhaps more important to ...?
Let's think about this new point.

Can I come in here?

Exactly! And can I just add that ....

You can interrupt to support speakers and develop ideas.

Would it be possible to have ten minutes' break? I have another meeting.

Try to avoid unnecessary interruptions.

I think we're forgetting that it's time for a coffee break.

Keep interruptions relevant.

http://access.englishcentral.com/compass/meetingsinterruptions

Fill in the blanks. Listen and check.

add	at once	superficially	in more depth

Mark: If I could just interrupt for a moment ...

Bob: I think Linda has made a good point. Did you want to _____ something, Mark?

Mark: Yes. I'd like to add namely that different clients have different needs. A few of the suggestions we've heard _____ acknowledge these differences. But I think if we explore these techniques _____, we'll find that they really make all the same assumptions about the needs of our clients.

Karen: May I just point out ...

Linda: Just a minute, Mark ...

Bob: One at a time, please. We can't all speak _____. Yes, Linda? ...

V O C A B U L A R Y

Find a word in the Vocabulary list with a similar meaning. Write the word.

1. at the same time   _____

2. break in   _____

3. deeper   _____

4. important   _____

5. use wisely   _____

P R A C T I C E

Match the questions or statements with similar meanings.

1. Did I make my point clear?
2. I just want to mention one thing.
3. If I could just finish.
4. May I interrupt?
5. Not everyone can speak at once.

a. Could I come in and say something?
b. Do you think everyone understood?
c. I was not done speaking.
d. Please let me make just one point.
e. We can't all comment at the same time.

7. Asking questions

NOUNS
device
impact

VERBS
follow
be with
elaborate
repeat
go over

ADJECTIVES
open
closed
factual
vital

ADVERBS
thoroughly
in other words

Check questions – we want to make sure people understand

Do you follow?
Do you see what I mean?
Are you with me?

Development questions – we want more information

Could you say a little bit more about that?
Would you elaborate on that a little?
Could you go into more detail about ...?
Can you give an example?

You need clarification

What exactly do you mean by ...?
What are you trying to say exactly?
Why do you feel that is important?

You need to hear a second time

I'm sorry, could you repeat that?
Could you go over that again, please?

You are listening

So you're worried about ....
If I understand you correctly, you're saying that ....
So, in other words, you think that ....

Open questions

Could you tell me ...?
I'd be interested to know ....
What sort of ...?

Closed questions

Do you plan to ...?
Is there ...?
Did you ...?
Are you going to ...?

Leading questions

Shouldn't we discuss ...?
Isn't it important to ...?
Can't we ...?

Factual questions

When will we begin production?
Who will lead the team?

Avoid too many closed questions.
They are limited and people will probably
only say "yes" and "no".

Leading questions.
These questions are a useful device to
add power to your ideas!

Meetings tip!
Asking questions is a vital communication skill.
By asking questions you clarify what is said and
explore all the items on the agenda thoroughly.

Fill in the blanks. Listen and check.

vital	elaborate	thoroughly	with me

Karen: This has had a huge impact on my sales over the last year.

Linda: I'm not sure I follow. Could you _____ on your closing technique?

Karen: I don't think it's _____ to go over the whole technique in detail at this meeting. The main point is that the overall approach brings a whole new dynamic to the company-client relationship. Are you _____ on that point?

Linda: In other words, you deal with clients on a much more personal level.

Karen: Exactly.

Bob: I'd be interested in exploring this idea more _____ at a later meeting.

V O C A B U L A R Y

Mark each question as either open or closed.

	OPEN	CLOSED
1. Are we going to vote on that issue?	( )	( )
2. What exactly are you saying?	( )	( )
3. Did you already go over the graph?	( )	( )
4. Is this a vital problem for our business?	( )	( )
5. What does the device do?	( )	( )

P R A C T I C E

Label each question according to what is asked for.

repeat	clarify	elaborate

1. Can you go over that one more time? _____

2. Would you say that again, please? _____

3. How could you explain that in simple terms? _____

4. Could you tell us a bit more about the project? _____

5. What did you mean by that? _____

8. Making decisions

More discussion

I still feel we need to discuss ... a little more.
I think we should have more information on ....
I would like to look more closely at ....
I still can't agree to ....

Referring to time

We're running out of time.
We don't have any more time to spend on this.
We are almost out of time.
We are really behind schedule.

Closing the discussion

I'm afraid that I'll have to bring this point to a close.
I think we've discussed everything.
I don't think there is any more to be said.

Focusing

I really would like a decision on this.
Can we try and come to a decision now?
Are we ready to make a decision?

Establishing consensus

Can we agree to ...?
Does everyone agree that we ...?
Can I take it that everyone is now happy with the decision?
Well, it seems that we are all agreed that ....

Voting

Can we have a quick show of hands?
All in favor? Those against?
The proposal is carried.
The proposal is rejected.

Confirming

So, we are going to ....
All right, we have decided to ....
Just to confirm, we will ....

Deferring

I think we will have to leave this until the next meeting.
Regarding ..., we don't have enough information about this.
We need more information on ....

Moving on

Great, now can we move on to ...?
All right, now we should turn to ....
Let's go on to ....

Establishing and
checking consensus

Making progress

D I A L O G http://access.englishcentral.com/compass/meetingsmakingdecisions

Fill in the blanks. Listen and check.

out of time	consensus	carries	reject

Bob: I wish we had more time to spend brainstorming ideas, but it's getting late. But before we are completely _____, I'd like to try and come to a _____ on the next step in implementing some of these ideas.

Linda: If possible, I would really like to see an outline of all of the ideas from this meeting before deciding on which ones to implement and which ones to _____.

Mark: I'm also in favor of that proposal.

Bob: Can I get a show of hands on that? All in favor? It looks like the idea _____. Karen will type up the outline from the minutes.

V O C A B U L A R Y

Circle the word that does not belong in each group.

1. go on   move on   put on   turn to
2. consensus   idea   proposal   suggestion
3. behind   delayed   late   rejected
4. check   confirm   defer   review
5. approve   carry   focus   pass

P R A C T I C E

Choose the word with a similar meaning as the underlined words.

1. Everyone <u>was in favor of</u> the new plan.

   a. deferred   b. discussed   c. said   d. supported

2. The chairman <u>threw out</u> most of the committee's proposals.

   a. carried   b. confirmed   c. rejected   d. showed

3. Let's have a <u>show of hands</u> to see if we are ready to close the meeting.

   a. point   b. proposal   c. schedule   d. vote

4. Now, I would like to <u>turn to</u> recommendations for changing our system.

   a. go on to   b. have time to   c. run out of   d. spend time

5. The six members of the committee could not reach <u>consensus</u>.

   a. agreement   b. deferring   c. discussion   d. progress

9. Closing a meeting

Vocabulary

NOUNS
contribution
copy
minutes
report

VERBS
call it a day
close
cover
declare
look into
sum up
summarize

ADJECTIVES
adjourned
constructive
formal
fruitful
inefficient
informal
pointless
productive
stimulating
unproductive

Completing the agenda

I think we've covered everything.
OK. That's everything on the agenda.
Is there anything else to discuss?

Summarizing

Before we close, I should summarize the main points.
We discussed ... items.
So, our ... [first / second] objective was to ....
To sum up, we have decided to ....

Delaying decisions

We'll leave this until a later date.
We need more time to make a decision on this.
We'll discuss this at our next meeting.

Everything is clear

OK, is that clear?
Does everyone agree?
Any final questions?

Final questions

Can I check just one thing?
One final question ....
Did we agree to ...?

Confirm new responsibilities

So, what's the next step?
Bob, could you let us have a report on ...?
Martha will look into the question of ....
Jack, you'll let us have a copy of the minutes?
You should have a copy of the minutes by ....

Next meeting

Can we set a time for our next meeting?
Is June 28th convenient as a date for another meeting?
I'll confirm the date and location by next week.

Closing the meeting

Thank you for coming and for your contributions.
It was a pleasure to see you all today.
OK. We can finish there.
Let's call it a day. [Informal]
I declare this meeting adjourned. [Formal]

Just a last thought. Did we agree on tea or coffee for the next meeting?

CHAIRMAN

Clarify important decisions

> **Checklist:**
> **Closing a meeting**
> Say that the agenda is finished.
> Check no-one has anything more to say.
> Summarize the meeting: objectives and results.
> Ask if all understand and agree with the results.
> Confirm new responsibilities from the meeting.
> Set a date for the next meeting.
> Thank people for coming.
> Close.

Let's call it a day.

What kind of meeting?

Useful	-	Useless
Constructive	-	A waste of time
Productive	-	Unproductive
Stimulating	-	Boring
Helpful	-	Pointless
Fruitful	-	Inefficient

Fill in the blanks. Listen and check.

sum up	contribution	minutes	productive

Bob: That covers everything I wanted to accomplish at this meeting. Just to _____, Karen will make sure everyone at this meeting gets a copy of the _____ outlining all of the ideas. Then we'll meet again next week and look into how some of the ideas can be implemented. I want to thank you all for your _____ of stimulating ideas. I thought this was a very _____ meeting. Let's call it a day, folks.

V O C A B U L A R Y

Find an adjective in the Vocabulary list with a similar meaning and write it in the blank.

1. casual   _____
2. closed   _____
3. helpful   _____
4. interesting   _____
5. without purpose _____

P R A C T I C E

Use the checklist and put the following sentences in order for closing a meeting (a=first, e=last).

_____ 1. That's what we've all agreed on, right?
_____ 2. That covers everything on our agenda.
_____ 3. Is there anything anyone would like to add before we close?
_____ 4. Then, to sum up, we'll take a formal vote on this proposal next week.
_____ 5. This meeting is officially adjourned.

10. Problem-solving meetings

NOUNS
deadline
heart
manpower
root

VERBS
anticipate
arise
be a result of
be caused by
be due to
confront
deal with
face
lead to
monitor
move up
overcome
postpone
put off
reschedule
result from
tackle

ADJECTIVES
ahead
behind
enormous
in time
massive
on time
perennial

What is the problem?

We are facing a problem with ....
We need to look at the question of ....
In this meeting I would like to raise the problem of ....
We must confront the problem regarding ....
A problem with ... has arisen.

Cause

The problem was caused by ....
The problem resulted from ....
The problem was a result of ....
It was due to ....

Brainstorming – "How can we solve this problem?"

Troubleshooting – "We can solve this problem by ...."

Handling problems – key terms
To solve – to find a solution to
To deal with – to tackle
To overcome – to get round ⎤ ... a problem
To avoid – to prevent

Deadlines
To meet a deadline
To respect a deadline ⎤ good
To go over a deadline
To miss a deadline ⎤ bad

To delay
To postpone ⎤ **LATER**
To put off

EARLIER To move up

Solving problems – action plan verbs

to change – to develop – to adjust – to improve – to increase –
to reduce – to review – to monitor – to reschedule – to remove –
to add – to refuse – to accept

Future problems?

I don't anticipate any problems with ....
... shouldn't create a problem.
... won't cause any difficulties.
... may lead to a few problems.

Time
On time:
We finished the project on time. = according to the schedule
In time:
He arrived at the meeting in time to have a coffee before the formal start. = with enough time

The **root** of the problem is ...
The **heart** of the problem is ...

communication
technical
SOURCE
time
financial
management
manpower

a bit of a
enormous
major
massive
KIND
minor
perennial
serious
little

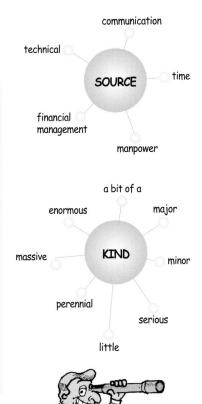

to monitor

to reduce

Schedule
We're on schedule.
We're behind schedule. (late)
We're ahead of schedule. (early)

D I A L O G http://access.englishcentral.com/compass/meetingsproblemsolvings

Fill in the blanks. Listen and check.

arose	anticipate	postpone	tackle

Linda: Hi, Sam. I was just calling to let you know my meeting at work finished on time and I'll be leaving the office soon.

Sam: Unfortunately, a problem _____ here, so I won't be able to leave for a while. In addition, we are facing a big deadline coming up Friday, so my boss wants to have a meeting tonight to _____ the root of the problem.

Linda: Then we'll have to _____ tonight's plans with Diane and her boyfriend.

Sam: Yeah, it might be better just to reschedule with Diane for next week. I _____ this problem will take a few days of working overtime to deal with.

V O C A B U L A R Y

Fill in the blanks to describe the type of problem.

communication	financial	manpower	technical	time

1. A minor _____ problem in the product was a result of bad manufacturing.

2. Our _____ problem was caused by a storm knocking down telephone lines.

3. Several delays in starting led to insufficient _____ to complete the project.

4. The company's _____ problems are due to bad investments by the CEO.

5. The factory's _____ problem resulted from the number of employees who quit after the factory was sold to a new corporation.

P R A C T I C E

Choose the best word to complete the sentence.

1. It's a _____ problem that won't be solved any time in the near future.
   a. ahead   b. behind   c. finished   d. perennial

2. Poor employee motivation is at the _____ of the problem.
   a. deadline   b. difficulty   c. heart   d. schedule

3. The best way to solve the problem is to _____ it head on.
   a. adjust   b. confront   c. postpone   d. reduce

4. Though the problem was initially small, it became _____ over time.
   a. enormous   b. improved   c. minor   d. perennial

5. We are _____ the problem to see if it gets worse.
   a. anticipating   b. facing   c. monitoring   d. tackling

11. Vocabulary building

Vocabulary

NOUNS
contingency
suggestion

VERBS
carry out
circulate
draw up
formulate
implement
put forward
reconsider
reject

ADJECTIVES
constructive
contingency
hasty
hidden
ingenious
joint
objective
realistic
ridiculous
ultimate
unanimous

If you wish to use English fluently and accurately, it is important to know how words combine in phrases and sentences. Here are some important word combinations connected with meetings.

A. Suggestion

To make a suggestion	A good suggestion
put forward – invite – welcome – reject	constructive – helpful – ridiculous – useful

He made a suggestion that we (should) reduce costs by 10%.
I have a suggestion concerning ....
At his suggestion, I have ....

B. Decision

To make a decision	A unanimous decision
come to – reach – reconsider - arrive at	joint – final – wise – fair – hasty – poor – quick

We made a decision to ....
We reached a decision about ....
It was a decision that was difficult to understand.

C. Plan

To present a plan	A detailed plan
approve – reject – carry out – drop - implement	ingenious – contingency – short-term long-term

The plan succeeded. • The plan failed. • Everything went according to plan.

D. Objective

To achieve an objective	A major objective
meet – set – state – agree to – formulate	primary – secondary – main – realistic – long-term – ultimate

E. Agenda

To draw up an agenda	A hidden agenda
put together – draft – put something on – circulate	

There are three items on the agenda. • This subject is very high on my agenda.

F. Opinion

To have an opinion	A personal opinion
hold – express – give – ask for – agree with	expert – honest – strong – objective – positive

In my opinion, ... • We had a difference of opinion • I'm of the opinion that ...

Ⓓ Ⓘ Ⓐ Ⓛ Ⓞ Ⓖ http://access.englishcentral.com/compass/meetingsvocabularybuilding

Fill in the blanks. Listen and check.

implement	unanimous	hasty	objective

Mark: I thought that was a very constructive meeting this afternoon.

Linda: I agree. I think Bob had a clear goal for the meeting. That helped a lot.

Mark: I think he also took an _____ view of the suggestions everyone put forward.

Linda: I'm glad there was a _____ decision to reconsider all the suggestions. After Karen circulates the minutes, we'll have the chance to formulate a realistic plan to _____ some of those suggestions in the future.

Mark: Yeah, I'm glad there wasn't a _____ decision made to just start trying the suggestions without a solid plan for carrying them out.

Ⓥ Ⓞ Ⓒ Ⓐ Ⓑ Ⓤ Ⓛ Ⓐ Ⓡ Ⓨ

Match the words with similar meanings.

1. hidden   **a.** clever

2. ingenious   **b.** final

3. joint   **c.** silly

4 ridiculous   **d.** together

5. ultimate   **e.** unseen

Ⓟ Ⓡ Ⓐ Ⓒ Ⓣ Ⓘ Ⓒ Ⓔ

Fill in the blanks with the correct preposition.

forward	out	up	to	with

1. The chair put _____ a suggestion, but the participants at the meeting rejected it.

2. It was very difficult to carry _____ the project according to the original plan.

3. The committee was responsible for drawing _____ an action plan.

4. Nobody agreed _____ her about how to solve the problem.

5. The group finally came _____ a decision after four hours of discussion.

12. Meetings at a glance

Vocabulary

NOUNS
agenda
decision
objective
opinion
progress
views

VERBS
add
cover
digress
go round
prepare
run over time
set a date
stick to
summarize

ADJECTIVES
clear
further
responsible

ADVERBS
partly

Introduction – the chair

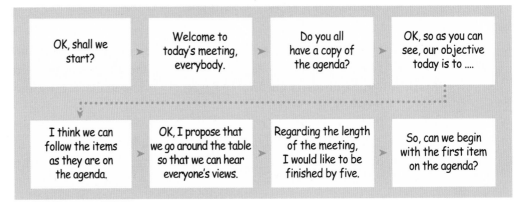

OK, shall we start?

Welcome to today's meeting, everybody.

Do you all have a copy of the agenda?

OK, so as you can see, our objective today is to ....

I think we can follow the items as they are on the agenda.

OK, I propose that we go around the table so that we can hear everyone's views.

Regarding the length of the meeting, I would like to be finished by five.

So, can we begin with the first item on the agenda?

The discussion

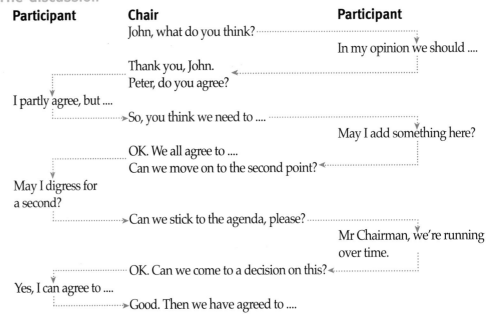

Participant	Chair	Participant
	John, what do you think?	
		In my opinion we should ....
	Thank you, John. Peter, do you agree?	
I partly agree, but		
	So, you think we need to	
		May I add something here?
	OK. We all agree to .... Can we move on to the second point?	
May I digress for a second?		
	Can we stick to the agenda, please?	
		Mr Chairman, we're running over time.
	OK. Can we come to a decision on this?	
Yes, I can agree to		
	Good. Then we have agreed to	

Ending – the chair

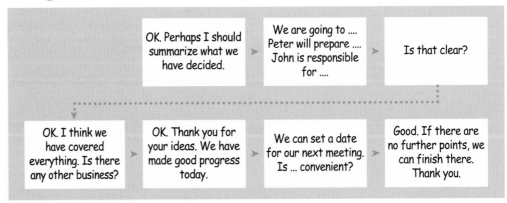

OK. Perhaps I should summarize what we have decided.

We are going to .... Peter will prepare .... John is responsible for ....

Is that clear?

OK. I think we have covered everything. Is there any other business?

OK. Thank you for your ideas. We have made good progress today.

We can set a date for our next meeting. Is ... convenient?

Good. If there are no further points, we can finish there. Thank you.

Fill in the blanks. Listen and check.

opinion	prepared	stuck to it	running over time

Bob: So, Linda, I'd like to get your _____ of how the meeting went.

Linda: I thought it went very well. You had a clear goal, and you _____.

Bob: Brainstorming suggestions was the only thing on the agenda.

Linda: I think it also helped that you _____ your own suggestion to start with. That got people thinking before you went around the table to hear other people's views. And I would add that your organization kept the meeting from _____.

Bob: Thanks, Linda. I feel we made real progress today with our sales strategy.

V O C A B U L A R Y

Fill in the blanks in this meeting's agenda.

date	decision	ideas	objective	points of view

Agenda: 1. State the meeting's _____

  2. Discuss different _____

  3. List the best _____

  4. Make a _____

  5. Set a _____ to begin

P R A C T I C E

Correct the mistake in each of the following sentences.

1. Before we vote, I want to summaries the key points related to this issue.

2. I part agree with you, but not entirely.

3. No one volunteered to be responsible of taking minutes at the meeting.

4. The chair did not think they could to cover all the items on the agenda.

5. If there are no farther points to discuss, we can adjourn this meeting.

13. Cross-cultural tips

There are many different types of business meetings. In addition, how participants behave will depend upon cultural background. Use the following as a checklist to help you prepare yourself for communicating in international meetings.

Preparation Some cultures...

- are happy with telephone meetings in preference to personal contact.
- expect extensive pre-meeting documentation and briefing information.
- prefer communication of prepared ideas to spontaneity during discussion.
- value fact over opinion.

Structure Some cultures...

- regard small talk as essential to establish the required personal relationship.
- prefer certain types of meetings (briefing) to others (problem solving).
- view informality as unprofessional.
- expect to work systematically on an agenda.
- work organically and value flexibility and digression.

Roles Some cultures...

- see the chair as controller and decision-maker rather than facilitator.
- prefer an individualist to a collectivist approach.
- expect important decisions will be made by **senior** personnel in the company.

Language and communication People can...

- find idiomatic language difficult. Keep it short and simple.
- be frustrated by native speaker domination. Allow others to speak.
- misunderstand silence: is it agreement, non-understanding, thinking time, boredom?
- be offended. Humor is often personal and culturally specific. Use with caution.

Time Some cultures...

- respect punctuality.
- are very concerned with deadlines.
- are flexible about time.

Decision-making Some cultures...

- prefer logic to imagination.
- prefer diplomacy to open disagreement.
- don't welcome interruption and contradiction.
- see directness as rude and unsophisticated.

Dress codes vary enormously

Non-verbal aspects People may...

- expect a formal dress code.
- see handshaking as the basis for establishing a personal relationship.
- see the exchange of business cards as important.
- have strong expectations about using first or family names. Family names are safer.
- mistake friendliness for unprofessionalism.

Fill in the blanks. Listen and check.

behave	diplomacy	business cards	offend

Mark: What was my most difficult meeting? Probably the contract meeting I attended on a business trip to Japan.

Linda: I bet that meeting required a lot of _____.

Mark: The hard part was trying to figure out how to _____.
It was very frustrating.

Linda: Did you do anything to _____ someone at the meeting?

Mark: I don't think so. But it was awkward greeting people by exchanging _____ instead of giving them a handshake. And there was a lot more silence at the meeting than I am used to. It was all very foreign to me.

V O C A B U L A R Y

Choose the word to complete the definition. Write the word in the blank.

collectively	individually	organically	silently	systematically

1. To work alone is to work _____.

2. To allow flexibility and spontaneity in work is to work _____.

3. To work as a group is to work _____.

4. To have a set procedure to follow is to work _____.

5. To work without speaking is to work _____.

P R A C T I C E

Choose the word that is similar in meaning to the underlined words.

1. He did <u>wide</u> research about the culture before he traveled there.

    a. extensive   b. frustrating   c. personal   d. senior

2. He thought her <u>casual behavior</u> was rather rude.

    a. diplomacy   b. domination   c. flexibility   d. informality

3. My <u>first choice</u> would be to meet later in the afternoon.

    a. opinion   b. preference   c. silence   d. spontaneity

4. The <u>argument</u> began because they didn't understand each other's cultures.

    a. collectivist   b. disagreement   c. facilitator   d. flexibility

5. The chairman's joke greatly <u>angered</u> her.

    a. offended   b. prepared   c. unprofessional   d. unsophisticated

14. Golden rules

NOUNS
authority
clarity
irrelevance
name card
objective
over-elaboration
pace
refreshments

VERBS
bully
dominate
guarantee
implement
impose
improvise
organize
pretend
react
review
slow down

ADJECTIVES
direct
flexible
sufficient

Practice and rehearse key English phrases.

Chairing

DO

- plan the meeting thoroughly: agenda – format – people – minutes.
- begin by reviewing objectives.
- encourage ideas from all the participants.
- listen: clarify, summarize and focus the discussion.
- impose control on strong personalities.
- respect time: maintain pace but slow down for analysis.
- guarantee a result: identify the issues and find consensus.
- summarize decisions at the end.
- implement any action plan and organize the next meeting.

DON'T

- forget the environment: you may need name cards, flipchart, refreshments.
- dominate and bully people with your authority.
- allow over-elaboration or irrelevance.
- postpone decisions too quickly to another meeting.
- close a meeting without reviewing decisions.

Participating

DO

- read the agenda before and bring supporting documentation.
- speak with sufficient volume and clarity for everyone to hear you.
- respect and support other speakers: develop their ideas.
- be flexible and willing to improvise.
- listen and check to make sure that you understand.
- give direct replies: don't digress.
- build to a consensus.

DON'T

- leave meetings to make 'important' phone calls.
- interrupt too much or disagree too strongly.
- react personally to differences of opinion.
- use over-complex language.
- pretend to understand.
- eave a meeting without clearly understanding the decision.

Fill in the blanks. Listen and check.

organize	authority	dominate	guarantees

Bob: The most important thing about chairing a meeting is to have clarity of purpose.

Linda: I can see how that can help the chair _____ the agenda.

Bob: And it can also help the chair keep the meeting on track. When discussion takes place, a clear objective _____ the chair can tell when topics of irrelevance are taking up too much time.

Linda: And that's when the chair needs to use her or his _____ to cut off the discussion and refocus the meeting.

Bob: Yes, but the chair shouldn't bully the participants or _____ the discussion.

V O C A B U L A R Y

Mark each idea as a good idea (DO) or bad idea (DON'T) for a meeting.

	DO	DON'T
1. As chair, impose authority so everyone follows a decision.	( )	( )
2. Pretend you understand if a topic is complicated.	( )	( )
3. When the meeting does not follow the agenda, improvise.	( )	( )
4. As chair, pay attention to the pace of the meeting.	( )	( )
5. Give participants sufficient time to share ideas.	( )	( )

P R A C T I C E

Who will prepare each thing? Write the correct word in the blank.

agenda	conference room	minutes	name cards	refreshments

1. Sue: _____ (the plan for the meeting)

2. Tom: _____ (badges for people to wear)

3. Mary: _____ (where the meeting will be held)

4. John: _____ (notes from the previous meeting)

5. June: _____ (snacks and drinks)

CHAPTER 4

English for Socializing

1. First meetings
2. Social phrases – responding
3. Talking about jobs
4. Talking about family and relationships
5. Talking about home
6. Talking about interests and sport
7. Talking about movies and stage shows
8. Talking about vacations
9. Talking about business environment
10. Talking about health and lifestyle
11. Making invitations
12. Eating out
13. Saying good-bye
14. Cross-cultural tips

1. First meetings

Vocabulary

NOUNS
appointment
journey
trip
visit
weather

VERBS
get down to business
have a chance
look around
manage
take a seat

ADJECTIVES
awful
chilly
damp
delayed
excellent
free
miserable
overcast
scorching

Other
on behalf of

At the reception desk	Receptionist
Hello, my name is .... I have an appointment with ... at	Please take a seat. I'll see if he's free.
Introducing yourself	**Responding to introductions**
Excuse me, are you ...? How do you do. I'm John. Welcome to New York. Let me introduce myself. My name is .... You must be .... Nice to meet you. I'm .... I don't think we've met. I'm	That's right. Pleased to meet you. Nice to meet you. I'm .... Hi. But please call me .... Sorry, I didn't catch your name.
Introducing another person	
May / Can I introduce you to .... Mr...., this is Mr. .... Have you met Mrs ...? Bob, do you know Bill?	 On behalf of our Chief Executive Officer, I'd like to welcome you to Alaska.
Polite offers	**Responding to polite offers**
May I take your coat? Do you need some help with that? Can I get you something to drink? Tea? Juice? Coffee? Regular or decaf? Do you take milk? Sugar?	Thank you, that's very kind of you. Thanks, but I think I can manage it. Tea would be great, please. Decaf, if you have it, please. Black with one spoon of sugar, thanks.

The host – small talk

Travel
When did you arrive? How was your journey?
Did you have a good trip?
Did you have any problems finding us?

I arrived yesterday evening.
Everything went fine. No problems.
The traffic was awful.
My flight was delayed a little.
I couldn't get a taxi.

Accommodation
Where are you staying?
How's the hotel?

I'm staying at the City Hotel downtown.
It's very comfortable.
The service is excellent.

Place
Is this your first visit to ...?
Have you had a chance to look around?
What do you think of ...?

I haven't had time to see anything yet.
This is my second time in ....
It seems to be a wonderful city.

Weather
How's the weather in ...?
Is the weather the same in ...?
I hope the weather is better in ....

Weather Words
It's freezing–cold–chilly–warm–hot–scorching.
It's pouring–raining–windy–cloudy–overcast–sunny.
It's humid–dry–wet–damp.
It's awful–terrible–miserable–beautiful–wonderful.
We are having a good–average–bad summer.
It's been a bad winter so far.
It's very changeable.

Closing the introduction
OK. Let's get down to business.

Fill in the blanks. Listen and check.

miserable	free	catch	look around

Linda: Good afternoon. I have an appointment with Mr. Miller.

Receptionist: Please, take a seat. Mr. Miller is taking a conference call at the moment ... (on phone) Mr. Miller, are you _____? ... You may go in now.

Miller: How do you do, Ms ... I'm sorry, I didn't _____ your name.

Linda: Linda Strait. Please call me Linda.

Miller: A pleasure to meet you, Linda. I hope you have a chance to _____ our beautiful city before you fly back. How was the flight coming here, by the way?

Linda: It was fine. I thought I might be late because the flight was delayed by the _____ weather back home. But the pilot somehow managed to make up the time.

V O C A B U L A R Y

Circle the word or phrase that does not belong in each group.

1. journey	person	trip	visit
2. awful	miserable	terrible	wonderful
3. catch	get	hear	manage
4. calm	cold	cool	chilly
5. behind	delayed	early	late

P R A C T I C E

Put the following sentences in logical order (a=First, e=Last).

_____ **1.** I'm sorry to hear that. But the weather should be nicer this weekend.

_____ **2.** Sorry. I thought you had been introduced. This is Steve.

_____ **3.** I'm sorry. I didn't catch your colleague's name.

_____ **4.** Traffic was awful because of the bad weather.

_____ **5.** It's a pleasure to meet you, Steve. How was your coming here?

2. Social phrases – responding

Vocabulary

NOUNS
a shame

VERBS
give a hand
have (got) a clue
kid
matter
mention
mind
take a break
worry

ADJECTIVES
annoying
possible
typical

Offering help
Would you like me to ...?
Shall I ...?
Can I give you a hand?

Responding
That would be great. Thank you.
No, it's OK. Thank you.
If you could, thanks.

Requesting
Could/can you ..., please?
*Would you mind -ing ...?
Do you think you could ...?

Of course, that's no problem.
*No, not at all.
I'm afraid I can't.

Asking permission
May/can I ...?
Is it OK if I ...?
*Do you mind if I ...?
Do you think I could ...?

Sure. Yes, of course./Yes, go ahead.
Certainly.
*Of course not.
Actually, I'm afraid it isn't possible to ....

*"Do you mind?" means "Are you unhappy?" so the answer must be "no."

Suggestions
I suggest that we meet later for a drink.
Why don't we meet later?
Shall we take a break?
Do you want a break?

Yes, great idea.
I'm afraid I can't.
Yes, OK. Let's do that.
I don't mind.
Sure, if you'd like one.

A thank you
Thank you very much for your help.

You're welcome.
Don't mention it.

Surprising news
The stock market rose ten percent this
    morning.

Really? You're kidding!
I don't believe it.

Bad news
I had to cancel our vacation to Thailand.
My aunt is sick.
The restaurant is closed.
It's just started to rain.

That's too bad.
What a shame. I'm sorry to hear that.
That's annoying.
Typical. I don't have an umbrella with me.

A difficult question
What is the population of New York?

To be honest, I'm not sure.
I couldn't even make a guess on that one!
I haven't got a clue!
It depends what you mean by ....

An apology
I'm very sorry about that.

It doesn't matter. Don't worry.
Never mind.

Fill in the blanks. Listen and check.

mind	annoying	shame	take a break

Miller: We've been at this all afternoon. Let's _____ and go out for coffee.

Linda: That sounds like a good idea.

Miller: I know a great coffee shop down the street if you don't _____ walking a bit.

Linda: Not at all. Oh! Look at the rain! It's pouring outside!

Miller: That's typical around here. It rains almost every day this time of year. It's a _____ you couldn't see the city in the spring. The weather is much nicer then.

Linda: But I don't have an umbrella or anything. How _____!

Miller: Don't worry. We keep extras here in the office.

V O C A B U L A R Y

Match the questions with the appropriate response.

1. Can I give you a hand with that?
2. Did you mean that seriously?
3. Is it OK if I smoke here?
4. Why don't we take a break?
5. Would you mind closing the window?

a. Great. I could use some coffee.
b. Thanks. I'd appreciate that.
c. No, I was just kidding.
d. Not at all.
e. I'm sorry. This is a "smoke-free" building.

P R A C T I C E

Choose the correct word to complete the definition. Write the word in the blank.

give a hand	hasn't got a clue	matters	never mind	typical

1. A person who doesn't know anything about a topic _____.

2. If something is important, it _____.

3. One way to tell someone to forget a request you made, is to say "_____."

4. Something that is common or ordinary is _____.

5. When you want to help someone, you can offer to _____ to them.

3. Talking about jobs

Vocabulary

NOUNS
base
client
consultant
downside
early retirement
lead time
quality control
range
salary
section

VERBS
apply for
be divided into
deal with
earn
join
lay off
manufacture
promote
provide
report
specialize
work for
work on

ADJECTIVES
above
below
freelance
immediate
in charge of
involved in
responsible for
stressful
under pressure
working on

What do you do?

I'm ....

I work in the Finance Department.
I work in a bank in New York.
I'm in marketing. I work freelance.
I'm a consultant.

What are your main responsibilities?

I'm **in charge** of marketing the product.
I'm **responsible for** developing our client base.
I **deal with** quality control.
I'm also **involved in** a project focused on personnel development.
At the moment I'm **working on** a project to improve lead times.

Who is your boss?

I report to Mr Lewis, who is my immediate boss.
So, above me there is Mr Lewis. Below me,
  there are five people who report to me.
My department is divided into five sections.
I work with a person from Thailand.

Who do you work for?

I **work for** New York Consultants.
It's a telecommunications company.
We **manufacture** electronic products.
The company **specializes** in financial services.
We **provide** a range of products.

What is your background?

I wanted a **career** in finance so I **studied** finance and economics in college. The first job I **applied for** was with ECO corporation in Tokyo. They recruited me in 1987. I **left** this company in 1989 and **joined** Harvard Finance in 1992. The company had a lot of problems and I was **laid off** in 1994. I joined my present company, Singapore Accounts, two years ago. I have worked for Singapore Accounts since 1996. It was a good move. I was **promoted** to Finance Director last year and I now **earn** a good **salary**. I'm currently **working on** a new financial accounting system. It will be ready soon. The downside of the job is that I **work long hours** and I only **get three weeks' vacation**. I'm always **under pressure** and sometimes it is a bit **stressful**. I also **spend a lot of time** traveling. I am now fifty-five and I am considering **taking early retirement** next year.

Word Checklist – Career

To study a subject at university	To earn a salary
To recruit a person	To get a vacation
To apply for a job	To work long hours
To leave a company	To be under pressure
To join a company	To be stressed out
To be laid off	To spend a lot of time doing something
To be promoted	To take early retirement

D I A L O G

 http://access.englishcentral.com/compass/talkingaboutjobs

Fill in the blanks. Listen and check.

salaries	stressful	applying for	freelance

Linda: This coffee shop is wonderful. Thanks for bringing me here.
Miller: My pleasure, Linda. So, Bob tells me you joined the company recently.
Linda: That's right. I started _____ jobs last January and was hired in March.
Miller: What did you do before that?
Linda: Before that I was a _____ consultant.
Miller: Really? I heard consultants earn great _____. Why did you quit that?
Linda: It was too _____ moving from job to job. I wanted steadier work. And I have found the work I'm involved in now is very interesting and exciting.

V O C A B U L A R Y

Who is the boss? Read the hints. Write the person's name in the correct box.

1. Nancy's immediate boss is a man.

2. Tom has worked with Charles for two years.

3. Nancy and Mary report to the sales manager.

4. Tom does not work in sales.

5. Alice is above Charles.

P R A C T I C E

Choose the best word to complete each sentence.

1. I'm expecting an important call from a _____ this afternoon.

   a. client   b. quality   c. range   d. salary

2. Someone from this office will be _____ to manager when Ron retires.

   a. earned   b. manufactured   c. promoted   d. provided

3. She was _____ to complete the project by the deadline.

   a. in charge   b. responsible   c. stressful   d. under pressure

4. We've looked at the benefits. Now, let's see the_____ of the recommendation.

   a. base   b. downside   c. retirement   d. section

5. Our company _____ in toys with educational value.

   a. applies   b. divides   c. joins   d. specializes

4. Talking about family and relationships

Name

My full name is William James Wells.
My first name is William.
My middle name is James.
My last name / family name / surname is Wells.

Status

You say	Male	Female
I'm single	bachelor	single woman
I'm engaged	fiancé	fiancée
I'm married	husband	wife
I'm divorced	ex-husband	ex-wife
I remarried	second husband	second wife

'Married or not married?'
Mr is for married and unmarried men.
Miss is for single women.
Mrs is for married women.
Ms is a term preferred by many women today. It can be used by married and unmarried women.

Stepfather - stepmother
The name for a parent of a second marriage.

> The term "partner" is common to refer to the person you live with.

A Love Story

We **first met** at work. We **got along** very well as we **had a lot in common** and so we soon started **dating**. After a year we decided to **get engaged**. We **got married** six months later. **We had our first child**, our son, in 1978 and a second child, our daughter, was born in 1981. **We have been together** for over twenty years now. Our son still **lives at home**. Our daughter **left home** last year to go to college.

Heart

Not A Love Story

We **first met** in 1991 and we **got married** six months later. We **had a son** soon after. **Things didn't really work out** between us and we **separated** in 1993. We finally **got divorced** in 1994. I **got custody** of our son. His father visits on weekends. I **remarried** last year and I'm very happy now with my **second husband**.

Broken heart

Single-parent family: A family where one parent brings up the child / children.
An only child: A child with no brothers or sisters.

Relations

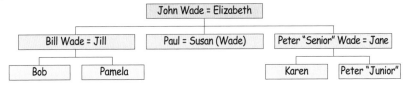

John and Elizabeth Wade are Bob's **grandparents**.
Elizabeth Wade is Paul's **mother-in-law**.
Jill is Paul's **sister-in-law**.
Peter "Senior" is Bob's **uncle**.
Pamela is Susan's **niece**.

John Wade is Paul's **father-in-law**.
Peter "Senior" is Paul's **brother-in-law**.
Susan is Bob's **aunt**.
Bob is Susan's **nephew**.
Bob and Karen are **cousins**.

http://access.englishcentral.com/compass/talkingaboutfamilyrelationships

Fill in the blanks. Listen and check.

| remarry | married | dating | separated |

Miller: Sorry about the interruption. That was my fiancée calling.

Linda: Your fiancée? I would have guessed from your age you were _____ already.

Miller: I was married for six years, but my wife and I _____ two years ago.

Linda: So you're not divorced yet?

Miller: No. I didn't see much use in getting a divorce until recently. I met a wonderful woman through a dating service. We've been _____ for several months, and now I've decided to _____. We got engaged two weeks ago.

Linda: Congratulations!

V O C A B U L A R Y

Fill in the blanks with the correct name of the relation.

1. _____ = your brother's wife

2. _____ = your father's sister

3. _____ = your grandmother's husband

4. _____ = your sister's son

5. _____ = your uncle's daughter

P R A C T I C E

Complete the information card with information about yourself.

> **Name:** _____
>   (first name)   (last name)   (middle initial)
>
> **Marital Status:**   Single   Married   Divorced   Separated
>
> **Number of children:** _____
>
> **Mother's maiden name*:** _____
>
> **Number of brother and sisters:** _____

* mother's last name before marriage

5. Talking about home

Vocabulary

NOUNS
bedroom
bungalow
carpet
central heating
childhood
cottage
country
duplex
fireplace
floor
kitchen
living room
location
mortgage
outskirts
region
suburbs
town
town house
villa
village
yard

VERBS
bring up
build
design
grow up
overlook
own
rent

ADJECTIVES
specific
surrounded by
tiled
wood

Types of home

A three-bedroom house / apartment
A duplex
A town house
A villa

A bungalow
A house in the suburbs
A cottage
A rented room

A bungalow

I **rent** my house. **The rent** is US$600 a month.
I **own** my house. **The mortgage** is US$650 a month.
I used to live in Chicago. I **moved to** New York last summer.
I **designed** and **built** the house myself.

Places in the home

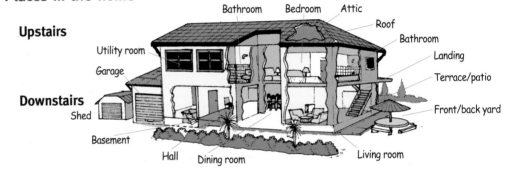

Upstairs
Utility room
Garage
Bathroom   Bedroom   Attic
Roof
Bathroom
Landing
Terrace/patio
Front/back yard

Downstairs
Shed
Basement
Hall   Dining room
Living room

Typical actions in the home

Bedroom: [a.m.]   wake up – turn off the alarm clock – get up – get dressed
Kitchen: have breakfast – do the cooking – do the dishes
Living room: watch TV – have a look at the newspaper – sit and relax
Yard: do the gardening – get some fresh air – cut the grass
Bedroom: [p.m.]   go to bed – set the alarm clock – go to sleep – dream

I don't like **carpets**. I prefer **wood** or **tiled floors**.
I don't like **central heating**. I prefer **fireplaces**.

Where is home?

As a child

I was born in a little **village** and I **grew up** there. I **spent a lot of my childhood** in the country, not in the **city**. We **moved to** a nearby **town** when I was fifteen. I'm glad I wasn't **brought up** in the city.

Location

I live on the outskirts of Chicago.
I live thirty kilometers from Kobe.
I live by the sea / on the coast.
I live just outside Los Angeles.
I live in the suburbs of Paris.
The house has a lovely view. It is surrounded by woods and it overlooks an old church.
Dayton isn't far from Cincinnati.
My town is to the north / south / east / west of New York. [specific location]
My town is in the north / south / east / west part of Japan. [country / region]

Where were you born?

Are you from Dallas originally?

Where is it exactly?

Where do you live?

D I A L O G http://access.englishcentral.com/compass/talkingabouthome

Fill in the blanks. Listen and check.

suburbs	region	mortgage	surrounded by

Linda: You mean you grew up in this town?

Miller: Basically. Actually, I was brought up in the _____, but I still consider this my hometown. And in all my years here, I've seen this town grow a lot.

Linda: I've heard that lots of people are moving to this _____ nowadays.

Miller: They sure are! This town used to be _____ fields and forests. Now it's all housing developments. Every year there's more and more construction on the outskirts of town. Housing prices are up, too. The _____ on the house I own would be twice today what I paid originally.

V O C A B U L A R Y

Look at "places in the home." Write where each person is probably doing the activity.

1. He is cooking spaghetti for lunch. He is in the _____.

2. She is mowing the grass. She is in the _____.

3. He is lying on the sofa watching TV. He is in the _____.

4. She is taking a nap. She is in the _____.

5. He is taking a shower. He is in the _____.

P R A C T I C E

Fill in the blanks in the following real estate advertisements.

carpet	fireplace	kitchen	overlooking	tiled	house

1. 2-bedroom _____
   Includes new _____ on
   the living room floor, a brick
   _____, and a spacious
   _____. Call for an
   appointment. 433-6900

2. Cute apartment _____
   downtown. Single bedroom with
   _____ floor in kitchen
   and bathroom.
   Rent $600/month.
   No pets. Call 762-5815

6. Talking about interests and sport

Vocabulary

NOUNS
antiques
bat
clubs
collector
course
court
field
free time
helmet
nil
racket
referee
sets
spectator
stadium
stick
table tennis
tie-break
tournament
track
umpire
weekend

VERBS
beat
can't stand
collect
don't care much for
enjoy
hate
like
lose
love
tie
win

ADJECTIVES
creative
spare
tied

Questions

What do you do in your spare/free time?
What do you usually do on the weekends?
Do you play any sports?
Are you interested in classical music?
Do you like walking?

I love ....
I really like ....
I enjoy ....
I quite like ....
I don't care much for ....
I don't really like ....
I can't stand ....
I really hate.....

Interests	
Outdoor	I go ... walking, climbing, fishing, hunting, camping, skiing
Games	I play ... chess, bridge, backgammon, poker
Collectors	I collect ... stamps, coins, antiques
Creative	I like... photography, painting
Subjects	I'm interested in ... politics, history, psychology, impressionism
Music	I play ... the guitar, the piano, the saxophone, in a band
Cultural	I like ... reading, classical music, ballet, opera, the theatre, art

Sports

Do you play?
Football, soccer, basketball, volleyball, golf, tennis, table tennis, squash, badminton, baseball, ice hockey, cycling

Results
To win /lose something: She won the match. – She lost the game/the tournament.
To beat /lose to someone: Graff beat Sanchez. – America lost to Brazil.
To be tied: It was a tie game./America was tied with Brazil.

Sports	Specific terms
Football	quarter, touchdown, tackle
Baseball	inning, homerun, pitch
Basketball	quarter, basket, dribble
Soccer	half, goal, shoot
Tennis	set, game, serve
Golf	round, hole-in-one, putt

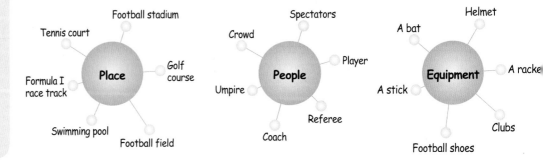

Place: Tennis court, Football stadium, Golf course, Formula I race track, Swimming pool, Football field

People: Crowd, Spectators, Player, Umpire, Referee, Coach

Equipment: A bat, Helmet, A stick, A racket, A racket, Football shoes, Clubs

Fill in the blanks. Listen and check.

courts	free time	courses	tournament

Miller: How do you spend your _____?

Linda: Most weekends, my husband and I work around the house or do shopping. But we both enjoy tennis. Sometimes we play at the tennis _____ by our house.

Miller: Oh, you're a tennis fan! Did you catch the last Wimbledon _____?

Linda: No, I didn't. I like playing tennis. I can't stand watching it on TV.

Miller: I understand. I love golf, but I don't care much for watching it.

Linda: I've heard some of the best golf _____ in the country are in this region.

Miller: You bet! I've played on most of them and lost every time! Ha ha!

V O C A B U L A R Y

Match the sport or activity with the equipment needed.

1. baseball   **a.** ball, bat, gloves, bases

2. golf   **b.** ball, goals, cleats (shoes)

3. soccer   **c.** balls, clubs, score pads

4. swimming   **d.** balls, rackets, net

5. tennis   **e.** pool, diving board, trunks

P R A C T I C E

Fill in the blanks in the following news article.

field	referee	spectators	Stadium	tie

Home Team Wins Championship!

All of the _____ at last Friday's sold-out game at Cooper _____ stood and cheered when our home team ran onto the _____. We were all so proud to see them play in the championship. But we were prouder to see them win! A penalty against the other team was called by a _____ in the last seconds of the game. Our team scored on the penalty shot to break the _____ and win the game!

7. Talking about movies and stage shows

Vocabulary

NOUNS
aisle
anti-climax
cast
climax
critic
hero
lead
performance
plot
review
row
scenery
soundtrack
standing ovation
star
subtitles

VERBS
dub
perform
play
premier
release
tour

ADJECTIVES
clever
dubbed
dull
gripping
moving
predictable
rave
reserved
shallow
supporting
touring
violent

Movies

What's on?

There are five new films showing at the movie theater.
The latest Spielberg film has just been released.
It was premiered in New York last month.

People

De Caprio played the lead in Titanic.
De Niro is a wonderful actor.
The real star of the film was the dog!
Jodie Foster won an Oscar for best supporting actress.
He was excellent as the action hero.

The content

The plot was very clever.
The film was set in the last century.
It was basically about a bank robbery that went wrong.
The soundtrack was excellent. I must get it on CD.
The film was dubbed. I prefer subtitles.

Types of movie

Western	War movie	Horror movie
Comedy	Thriller	Science fiction movie
Romance	Action movie	Adventure movie

What did you think?

The critics gave it rave reviews.

It has been getting poor reviews.

Stage shows/theater

I have reserved seats.
The play was by Shakespeare.
It is being performed by a touring company.
The whole cast was excellent.
It was a wonderful performance.
The scenery was a little dull.
The audience gave a standing ovation at the end.
It is one of the longest running shows in New York.

Hollywood blockbuster
Rocky 28

Who was the film directed by?

The director was Tarantino.

#$%^69&!
[]##@&!

There was a lot of bad language.

I don't like musicals.

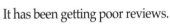
Seats   Row   Aisle

Where are we sitting?

Positive comments	Negative comments
It was moving.	It had a lot of bad language. And was very violent!
It was powerful.	It was a little shallow. Very disappointing.
It was gripping.	It was a little predictable.
It had a happy ending.	The ending was a bit of an anti-climax.
It was good fun.	It was slow. Very boring.

Fill in the blanks. Listen and check.

performance	lead	premier	reviews

Linda: I noticed signs around town advertising the touring production of the musical *Ghost of the Opera House.*

Miller: Yes, it's in town right now. Have you seen it? I caught the _____ of the show on Broadway a few years ago.

Linda: Really? You saw it when Vera Wilson played the _____? I heard that was an excellent production. The critics gave it rave _____.

Miller: It was great. The plot was predictable, but the whole cast gave an outstanding _____. And the scenery in the show was amazing!

VOCABULARY

Find a noun in the Vocabulary list to complete the definitions.

1. The words on the screen during a foreign movie are the _____.

2. A famous actor or actress playing the lead is called a _____.

3. An album with all of the music from a movie is the _____.

4. The man who saves everyone is the _____.

5. The highest or most exciting part of a story is the _____.

PRACTICE

Fill in the blanks in the following theater ticket using the words below.

aisle	performance	reserved	row	seat

All-Stars Touring Company and Theater Productions

proudly presents:

The Ghost of the Opera House

1. _____ date and time: Saturday, June 12, 7:30 PM

2. _____ seating: Balcony   3. _____ 4

4. _____ CC   5. _____ 7

Please keep ticket stub to enter theater after intermission.

8. Talking about vacations

Vocabulary

NOUNS
cabin
castle
cathedral
excursion
ferry
fountain
gallery
monument
night-life
sights
statue
temple
tour
tourist attractions

VERBS
book
drive
fly
get away
get lost
go camping
have a look around
look around
rent
stay
travel around

ADJECTIVES
cobbled
congested
cosmopolitan
dynamic
hilly
lively
marvelous
picturesque
quaint
touristy

Where did you go?

We stayed in a hotel.
We travelled around and stayed in guest houses.
Every year we like to get away and rent a cabin near the beach.
We booked a time-share.
We went camping.

Camping is fun!

How did you get there?

We flew to Argentina.
We drove through the States.
By boat / ferry / car / train

How long did it take to get there?

A long time.

What was it like?

The place
It is industrial / cosmopolitan / dangerous / violent /
safe / dynamic / lively / quiet / sleepy / noisy /
interesting / quaint / picturesque / boring / polluted /
clean / congested / touristy / packed.
The night-life is great.

The geography
It's flat / hilly / mountainous.
The climate is marvellous.
The scenery is wonderful.
A river / A lake / The sea / The ocean
The country / countryside
The environment

It's picturesque.

What did you see?

Did you see the sights?
What are the main tourist attractions?
What is there to do there?
We did some sightseeing.
We went on a sightseeing tour.
We had a guided tour.
We went on an organized tour / excursion to ....
We went to the beach and did some sunbathing.
If you go, it is really worth having a guided tour.

The open-top bus tour was great.

The sights
A science / natural history / social history museum
An art gallery / A monument / A statue / A cathedral /
A temple / A fountain / A castle
The city is famous / well-known for ....
Narrow / cobbled streets

A lovely castle.

We had a great time!

We put our feet up and relaxed.
We looked around / had a look around.
We took a lot of photographs.
We got lost several times.

We enjoyed the peace and quiet.

D I A L O G http://access.englishcentral.com/compass/talkingaboutvacations

Fill in the blanks. Listen and check.

quaint	cabin	touristy	camping

Linda: The last time we had a vacation, my husband and I went _____.

Miller: I haven't been camping in ages. How was it?

Linda: Marvelous. We stayed near an area that is a ski resort in winter, but we were there in the summer. There was a _____ little town in the valley at the base of the ski slopes. It was a little _____, but very picturesque.

Miller: Did you rent a _____ there?

Linda: No, we camped in a tent. We spent most of our time hiking in the mountains, but on several evenings we went into town to look around and do some shopping.

V O C A B U L A R Y

Match the adjective with the noun it usually modifies.

1. cobbled   **a.** city

2. congested   **b.** landscape

3. cosmopolitan   **c.** night-life

4. dynamic   **d.** street

5. hilly   **e.** traffic

P R A C T I C E

Choose the best word to complete the sentence.

1. She wanted her picture taken by the _____ of Abraham Lincoln.

    a. cathedral   b. excursion   c. statue   d. tour

2. The guide urged the tourists to throw a coin into the _____ and make a wish.

    a. cabin   b. fountain   c. monument   d. temple

3. We took a _____ to visit the island.

    a. ferry   b. gallery   c. sight   d. monument

4. You should _____ your reservations now because the resort fills up fast.

    a. book   b. drive   c. rent   d. stay

5. The old _____was owned by a rich family, not a king.

    a. castle   b. excursion   c. temple   d. tourist

9. Talking about business environment

Vocabulary

NOUNS
competitor
core business
diversification
forecast
inflation
interest rate
investment
joint venture
mission
productivity
recession
recovery
share
taxes
trade
turnover
unemployment

VERBS
abandon
benchmark
boom
deregulate
downsize
merge with
outsource
privatize
relocate
restructure
slump
soar
subsidize
suffer
tailor
take over

ADJECTIVES
booming
core
external
internal
joint

The economy

Inflation		increased	a little.
Unemployment	**has**	gone up	a lot.
Investment			
The balance of trade			
Interest rates	**have**	decreased	slightly.
Exports – Imports		gone down	significantly.

We are seeing signs of a recovery.

Things are picking up.

The economy is booming.

We are suffering a recession.

The company

Turnover	went up	went down	last year.
Market share	rose	fell	
The share price			
Productivity	soared		in 2001.
Sales	slumped		
Prices			

Corporate strategy

We have **taken over** a smaller company.
We are planning **to merge with another** company.
We are going **to relocate** our manufacturing to China.
We are planning **a joint venture** in Beijing.
We are **focusing on core business**.
We have **abandoned diversification**.
We **tailor** our products to **customer needs**.
Our **mission** is to be **market leader** by 2005.

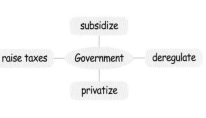

subsidize

raise taxes — Government — deregulate

privatize

Management – buzz words

Downsizing	making the company smaller and more efficient
Outsourcing	an external company provides an internal service
Restructuring	reorganizing
Benchmarking	comparing your performance with your competitors'

objective goal aim target $200m

The future

What is the forecast?
What do you expect in terms of ....

What do you think?

Do you agree?

Opinions
I think that ....
In my opinion ....
As I see it ....

Agree
I agree with you.
Definitely.
I think so too.

Disagree
I'm not sure.
Yes, but ....
I see what you're saying but ....

What is your opinion?

D I A L O G http://access.englishcentral.com/compass/talkingaboutbusinessenvironment

Fill in the blanks. Listen and check.

downsize	recession	outsourcing	unemployment

Linda: Do you think this _____ can get much worse?

Miller: On the contrary! I see signs of a recovery. The inflation rate has been steadily declining. And the _____ rate is also low.

Linda: But I've also heard reports that lots of companies will continue to _____ over the next few years.

Miller: That may be true, but I don't think the recession is the cause. Companies are restructuring and laying off people in redundant positions. And they're also _____ more work, so they need fewer permanent staff on the payroll.

V O C A B U L A R Y

What kind of economic problem is being described? Write the word in the blank.

downsizing	falling market	inflation	unbalanced trade	high unemployment

1. "The company is laying off 500 employees!" _____

2. "Shares are down 10 points!" _____

3. "Prices are on the rise!" _____

4. "We're importing more than we're exporting!" _____

5. "Too many people are out of work and can't find jobs!" _____

P R A C T I C E

Correct the mistake in each of the following sentences.

1. The bank is offering a very good interesting rate on loans.

2. The company wanted to take along its competitor, but it didn't have the funds.

3. Both the economy and the population were boomed in the 1950s.

4. The smaller company merged to the larger company last year.

5. The two companies proposed to undertake a joined venture.

10. Talking about health and lifestyle

NOUNS
a cold
a concussion
a hangover
a heart attack
a temperature
aspirin
asthma
blood pressure
blood test
bruise
cancer
cholesterol
dentist
diet
fever
food poisoning
hay fever
injection
pain
pharmacy
prescription
sore throat
stitches
the flu
weight

VERBS
break
burn
come down with
cut
cut down on
develop
diagnose
give up
knock unconscious
put on weight
scratch
suffer from
twist
watch

ADJECTIVES
allergic
fit
healthy
positive
sore
unconscious
upset

What's the matter?

I don't feel very well.
I've got a cold.
The baby had a fever.
I'm suffering from hay fever.
I have a hangover.
I've come down with the flu/a cold.

I feel sick/ill.
I have the flu.
I have a sore throat.

I have high blood pressure.

I have a temperature.
I have a upset stomach.
I'm allergic to peanuts.

Help!

I need an aspirin.
I must go and see a dentist.
Do you have anything for a headache?
I have a pain in my chest.
I think I should see a doctor.
I should go to the pharmacy and get some medicine.
I hope the doctor will give me a prescription.

Injuries

I cut my finger quite badly.
I twisted my ankle.
I had a concussion.
I had a bad bruise.

The cat scratched me.
I broke my leg.
I burnt my hand.
I knocked myself unconscious.

I had to go to hospital and have an injection.
I had blood tests.
I got a deep cut and needed ten stitches.
It was very painful.
It hurt.
She hurt herself quite badly.

This won't hurt!

Serious illness

I think I have food poisoning.
I sometimes suffer from asthma.
I had a heart attack.
She died from lung cancer.
He has been diagnosed HIV positive.
    He hasn't developed AIDS yet.

slim - thin - overweight - fat

Fitness and weight

I used to be really fit. But I'm not in very good shape now.
I'm really out of shape.
I try to keep to a healthy diet.
I've got to lose some weight.
I've put on a bit of weight recently.
I have to watch my weight.
I'm trying to give up smoking.
I've cut down on meat. My cholesterol level is too high.

You should watch your weight!

D I A L O G http://access.englishcentral.com/compass/talkingabouthealthandlifestyle

Fill in the blanks. Listen and check.

prescription	diagnosed	food poisoning	come down with

Miller: I hate traveling for business. I always seem to _____ something.
Linda: I've heard it's easy to catch a cold from flying.
Miller: A cold wouldn't bother me. When I get sick, it's worse than that. Like on my last business trip, I got _____!
Linda: That's terrible! Are you sure it wasn't just an upset stomach?
Miller: No, it was food poisoning. At first I thought it was the flu, so I went to the doctor. But he _____ it as severe food poisoning. Luckily, he gave me a _____ that worked great and I could still get some work done.

V O C A B U L A R Y

Circle the word that does not belong in each group.

1. aspirin   bruise   injection   stitches
2. cholesterol   cold   fever   flu
3. dentist   doctor   hangover   pharmacist
4. allergy   asthma   hay fever   temperature
5. fit   healthy   slim   sore

P R A C T I C E

Fill in the blanks in the following memo.

diagnosed	heart attack	knocked unconscious	sore throat	suffering from

To: The Factory Manager
From: Joe Workman
RE: Accident Report

Dear Sir:

This is the report of last Tuesday's accident. One of the workers reported he was _____ an illness earlier that day. He complained of a _____ and slight headache. After lunch, he became dizzy and fell down. He hit his head on a large machine and was _____. There were rumors that he had a _____, but this is not true. The worker was sent to the doctor and was _____ with the flu. He will return to work next week.

11. Making invitations

Vocabulary

NOUNS
appointment
baby sitter
couple
invitation
jacket
map
tie

VERBS
accept
arrange
confirm
decline
invite
join
look forward to
recommend
take a taxi
wonder

ADJECTIVES
delighted
early
fine
informal
late
later
over-dressed
polite

ADVERBS
exactly
fairly

Inviting

We'd like to invite you to dinner.
Would you like to come to dinner?
We were wondering whether you
    could come to dinner.
How about dinner?

Responding

Accepting
Thank you ....
I'd love to.
That would be nice.
I'd be delighted.
I'll have to arrange a baby sitter.

Declining
I'd love to, but ....
I'm sorry; but I've got another appointment.
I'm afraid I can't come. I'm going to ...

Time

Would Tuesday evening be okay?
What's a good time? Shall we say 7 o'clock?
Is 7 too early?
Let's say between 8 and 8:30.

Place

Where do you live exactly?
What's the best way of getting there?
I'd recommend that you take a taxi.
I'll send / give you a map.

Number

There'll just be the six of us.
We've invited a few friends.
There'll be six people there.
There will be a couple I know from ....

He's a little over-dressed.

Formality

What should I wear? Jacket and tie?
It will be fairly informal.

Confirming

So, that's 7:30 on Friday.
Let me just confirm that, Friday at 7:00 at your place.
I'll look forward to it.
Don't be late!

Cultural note:
It may be considered polite to give
a reason why you cannot accept an
invitation when you decline one.

D I A L O G http://access.englishcentral.com/compass/makinginvitations

Fill in the blanks. Listen and check.

wondering	delighted	recommended	looking forward to

Miller: Every Friday after work, a group from the office goes out for Happy Hour. I was _____ if you'd like to join us this evening.

Linda: I'd be _____. Thank you.

Miller: Happy Hour starts at 5, we'll leave the office a little early. Say 4:50?

Linda: That sounds fine with me. Where exactly do you go?

Miller: There is a bar and grill across the street that an old friend _____ to me. The food there is great and the atmosphere is very relaxed and informal.

Linda: Great! I'm _____ it.

V O C A B U L A R Y

Did the person accept the invitation? Check "accept" or "decline" for each sentence.

	ACCEPT	DECLINE
1. I would be delighted.	( )	( )
2. Thank you for asking, but I can't.	( )	( )
3. I'm afraid I don't have time to find a babysitter.	( )	( )
4. That sounds fine with me.	( )	( )
5. I'm sorry. I won't be able to make it.	( )	( )

P R A C T I C E

What is the purpose of each sentence? Write the correct label in the blank.

offering an invitation	setting the time	giving directions
predicting the number		explaining formality

1. Four other couples are coming, so please bring your husband. _____

2. I wanted to invite you to a party this weekend. _____

3. If you wear a suit and tie, you'll probably feel over-dressed. _____

4. The map shows how to get to my house. _____

5. We have to meet early, around eight in the morning. _____

12. Eating out

Vocabulary

NOUNS
bake
dessert
eggplant
grill
lamb
main course
oyster
present
receipt
shrimp
specialty
starter
veal
wine
wine list
zucchini

VERBS
give a ride
have over
mention
offer
order
recommend

ADJECTIVES
bitter
bland
delicious
fatty
raw
spicy
tasty
tender
vegetarian
wonderful

Arriving for dinner	The host
I've brought you a present. These are for you. You have a lovely house.	Thank you. That's very kind of you. Thank you. These are wonderful. Thank you. It's nice of you to say so.
During dinner	**The host**
It looks wonderful. Actually, I'm driving. That would be nice, thank you.	I hope you like it. Can I offer you more wine? More wine?
After the meal	**The host**
That was very good. Thank you for a wonderful evening.	Thank you. / Don't mention it. It was good to have you over.
No, thanks. But it was delicious. If it's no trouble. Thank you. Thank you very much.	Would you like some more? Should I call you a taxi? Can I give you a ride home?

Food

Meat
Beef Lamb
Pork Veal
Chicken Turkey

Vegetables
Beans Potato
Peas Cabbage
Eggplant Zucchini
Onion Corn

Ways of cooking
Boil Bake Grill
Fry Roast

Seafood
Shrimp Oyster
Salmon Lobster

In the restaurant

As a starter could I have ....
As a main course I'd like ....
Can you recommend anything?
Do you have anything vegetarian?
As a dessert I'll have ....
Could we see the wine list?
May I have a receipt?
Do you take American Express?
It was very nice, thank you.

Are you ready to order?
Is everything alright?

Can I have the check, please?

This is a local speciality. Raw beef!

Steak: rare / medium / well-done

How was the food?

Tasty
Tender
Delicious

Sweet
Spicy

Bland
Fatty
Bitter

D I A L O G http://access.englishcentral.com/compass/socializingeatingout

Fill in the blanks. Listen and check.

| wine | delicious | tasty | vegetarian |

Miller: How are you enjoying the Happy Hour, Linda?
Linda: It's wonderful! All of the food is _____.
Miller: Yeah. My favorites are the stuffed eggplant and cocktail shrimp.
Linda: The grilled zucchini is also very _____.
Miller: I noticed you didn't try the chicken wings. Are you a _____?
Linda: No, but I try to avoid fatty foods. And besides, they looked really spicy.
Miller: We should order drinks. How about some _____, Linda? Here is the wine list . . .

V O C A B U L A R Y

Label the parts of the menu. Write the correct word in the blanks.

| Desserts | Grill | Main Course | Starters | Wine List |

1. _____
Nachos
Buffalo Wings
Cheese Fries
Potato Skins

2. _____
Broiled Salmon
Lamb Chops
Baked Lasagna

3. _____
BBQ Chicken
Sirloin Steak
Shrimp on the Barbie

4. _____
House Red or White
Champagne

5. _____
Cheesecake
Ice Cream

P R A C T I C E

Circle the word with a similar meaning as the underlined words.

1. I need a <u>copy of the bill</u> to give to my company.
   a. course   b. receipt   c. specialty   d. veal

2. Did she <u>say briefly</u> who will be attending the party?
   a. mention   b. offer   c. order   d. recommend

3. The food was <u>tasteless,</u> so he added more spices.
   a. bitter   b. bland   c. raw   d. tender

4. The <u>gift</u> is very nice, but you really didn't have to get me anything.
   a. eggplant   b. oyster   c. present   d. roast

5. May I <u>suggest</u> the stuffed mushrooms with dipping sauce?
   a. have over   b. order   c. recommend   d. ride

13. Saying good-bye

Vocabulary

NOUNS
business card
comment
e-mail address
flight
home number
pleasure

VERBS
appreciate
contact
give a call
have (something) on one
keep in touch
leave
miss
reach
take care

ADJECTIVES
pleased
safe
useful

ADVERBS
carefully

Time to go

I'm afraid I'll have to go, otherwise I'll miss my flight.
I really should leave now.
I should be thinking about going.
OK. I'd better be off.

Positive comments	Response
It's been great working with you.	The same for me.
We've had a wonderful time.	I'm glad you found it interesting.
I really appreciate	No problem. I hope it was useful.
Everything was great.	I'm pleased you enjoyed it.

More comments

On behalf of us all, I'd like to say ....
It's going to be sad to see you go.
We'll all be sorry to see you leave.

Future contacts

I hope we'll see you again soon.
I'm sure we'll be seeing each other again very soon.
I look forward to seeing you next month.
Keep in touch.
Give me a call next time you are in ....

Contact numbers

Let me give you my business card.
Do you have my phone number?
Can I give you my office and e-mail address?
I don't have a card on me right now.
I'll give you my phone number.
You can reach me at ...
Let me give you my home number.

Goodbye

Final comments	Final responses
Have a safe journey!	Thanks.
Drive carefully!	I will.
Have a good trip!	I hope so.
Have a good weekend!	You too.
Take care!	Same to you
Bye!	Goodbye.

Take care!

Note
Saying e-mail addresses: @ = we say 'at'
                . = we say 'dot'

Travel
A: When is your flight?
B: 10 o'clock.
A: How long does the journey take?
B: Around three hours.
A: How much is the taxi fare?
B: About $40.
A: Do I need to confirm my flight?
B: Yes, you must.
A: How long does it take to get to the airport?
B: Around half an hour.

D I A L O G http://access.englishcentral.com/compass/socializingsayinggoodbye

Fill in the blanks. Listen and check.

pleasure	miss	appreciate	keep in touch

Linda: Look at the time! I'd better leave soon or I'll _____ my flight.

Miller: It's been a _____ working with you over the past few days, Linda.

Linda: I learned a lot while I was here. I think the trip was very useful. I really _____ everything you've done for me.

Miller: I'm sure we'll meet again. You have my business card with my e-mail address. Write or give me a call anytime.

Linda: Thanks. I will _____.

Miller: Have a safe trip back!

V O C A B U L A R Y

Match the sentences with similar meanings.

1. Have a safe trip.

2. I really appreciate it.

3. Let's keep in contact.

4. Use this phone number to call me.

5. I'm pleased it was useful for you.

a. I want to keep in touch with you.

b. I'm glad you got something out of it.

c. Take care.

d. Thank you.

e. You can reach me at this number.

P R A C T I C E

Correct the mistake in each of the following sentences.

1. I don't have a pen. Can I lend yours?

2. It will take about to thirty minutes to get there.

3. I hope you are having a good time next weekend.

4. My flight is departed at noon.

5. I need confirm my flight later this week.

14. Cross-cultural tips

Vocabulary

NOUNS
agreement
animation
behavior
complexity
connection
directness
disagreement
expression
gesture
handshake
hierarchy
honesty
hospitality
humor
impact
misunderstanding
personal space
posture
professionalism
proximity
punctuality
rudeness
seniority
sensitivity
stance
stereotype

VERBS
avoid   kiss
bond   respect
consider   shake hands
exchange   touch
interpret

ADJECTIVES
appropriate   personal
explicit   physical
facial   prescriptive
genuine   relative
implicit   taboo

To avoid cultural misunderstandings it is important to **CONSIDER** the impact your behavior will have on others and your sensitivity to others' behavior.

Body Language: Consider ....

The role of the handshake
The importance of eye contact
Communication through stance and body posture
The impact of facial expression
The degree of animation and gesture
Personal space: relative proximity
The level of physical contact such as kissing and touching

When do you shake hands?

Formality: Consider ....

The use of titles and names
How directness is interpreted
Dress codes
The exchange of business cards
Seniority: age and place in the hierarchy
The danger of humor

Dress appropriately.

Language and conversation: Consider ....

Small talk: bonding or a lack of professionalism
What is silence –agreement, disagreement, interest, lack of interest?
Which topics are taboo? Is work a conversation topic?
Is directness interpreted as honesty or rudeness?
The complexity of your language

That's a terrible tie!

Directness is not always appreciated.

Invitations: Consider ....

The appropriate level of hospitality
What to wear / When to arrive / Gifts to bring
Who pays: implicit or make it explicit
Appropriate places for entertainment
Are invitations genuine or just polite?

Please don't make me sing!

Time: Consider ....

What is the working day?
When are meal times?
What is the attitude to waiting?
Is punctuality important?
Are deadlines respected?
What is work time and what is personal time?

Dinner is served!

Society: Consider ....

Your knowledge: how much do you know about the country?
The relative roles of men and women
The danger of responding to stereotypes
The importance of personal connections: who you know

No! After you!

The world is changing!

D I A L O G

 http://access.englishcentral.com/compass/englishforsocializingcrossculturaltips

Fill in the blanks. Listen and check.

hierarchy	behavior	stereotype	sensitivity

Sam: Welcome home, honey! How was your trip?

Linda: It was very good. It gave me a new perspective on the _____ of managers.

Sam: What do you mean?

Linda: Mr. Miller has a very interesting attitude regarding his position. The office _____ is the same, but he seems to have a much closer personal bond with his employees. And he has a genuine _____ and respect for how employees divide their work time and personal time.

Sam: Sounds like he really doesn't fit the manager _____ at all.

V O C A B U L A R Y

Fill in the blanks with the correct word.

dress code	eye contact	facial expressions	personal space	small talk

1. Polite discussion between strangers or acquaintances is called _____.

2. Rules limiting what people can or cannot wear are called a _____.

3. Smiling and frowning are two examples of _____.

4. The distance a person likes to keep from other people is called _____.

5. When you look in someone's eyes, you make _____ with the person.

P R A C T I C E

Find a noun in the Vocabulary list to match each definition. The first letter is a hint.

1. P _____ - acting in a responsible and businesslike way

2. H _____ - always telling the truth

3. P _____ - being on time

4. D _____ - getting straight to the point

5. H _____ - making guests feel at home

CHAPTER 5

English for Negotiating

1. What makes a successful negotiation?

Vocabulary

NOUNS
advantage
agenda
conflict
deal
documentation
expectation
failure
framework
negotiation
outset
party
position
priority
procedure
relationship
series
statement
strategy
timetable

VERBS
bargain
extend
gather
inform
rehearse
settle
specify
state
stress

ADJECTIVES
constructive
firm
flexible
mutual
specific
to the point

ADVERBS
initially
positively

A definition

A negotiation is a meeting or a series of meetings in which the parties need each other's agreement to reach a specific objective which is to their mutual advantage. Do you agree?

Checklist – Effective Negotiating

Planning
- Read and gather pre-negotiation documentation
- Clarify important questions prior to the negotiation
- Know the other party: business and culture
- Decide objectives, strategy and agenda
- Specify roles and responsibilities within the team
- Inform people about date, location, and time
- Prepare and rehearse your opening statement

Clarify roles and strategy with your team!

Beginning the negotiation
- Create a positive atmosphere quickly
- Respect cultural expectations of behavior
- Establish a framework: agenda, procedure, roles
- Agree on a timetable
- State your position
- Stress common interests

During the negotiation
- Listen and clarify the objectives of the other party
- Check to make sure they understand you
- Focus initially on areas of agreement
- Make constructive proposals
- Be clear, firm and to the point
- Handle conflict positively
- Be creative and flexible when bargaining
- Reach a position of mutual advantage
- Establish a positive working relationship at the outset.

Establish a positive working relationship at the outset.

Ending the negotiation
- Summarize and confirm the deal
- Clarify future responsibilities
- End positively

After the negotiation
- Recognize successes
- Learn from failure and improve for next time
- Build up and extend the new relationship

Be flexible when bargaining.

The Negotiating Process

Greetings and positive opening ➤ Reviewing and agreeing on the agenda ➤ Establishing positions ➤ Clarifying priorities ➤ Making proposals ➤ Bargaining ➤ Handling conflict ➤ Settling ➤ Summarizing ➤ Closing

Fill in the blanks. Listen and check.

bargaining	extend	initially	procedure

Bob: I have a contact negotiation coming up this week, Linda. It might be a good idea for you sit in to see the _____.

Linda: That sounds very interesting. Who is the other party in this negotiation?

Bob: One of our suppliers. The company wants to renegotiate the contract we _____ signed with them.

Linda: What kind of deal are they looking for?

Bob: I was informed that the company will only _____ their contract with us if we agree to pay them a higher fee. They didn't specify how much, so the agenda of the negotiation will include _____ on the new fee.

V O C A B U L A R Y

Fill in the blanks with the correct word.

advantage	expectation	priority	strategy	timetable

1. Your _____ is something in your favor.

2. Your _____ is the first thing or the most important thing.

3. Your _____ is the schedule you hope to follow.

4. Your _____ is your idea or hope for how the meeting will go.

5. Your _____ is your plan for negotiating.

P R A C T I C E

Put the steps in order for a successful negotiation (a=first, e=last).

_____ 1. Close the meeting positively.

_____ 2. Confirm the terms of the deal before signing.

_____ 3. Establish the agenda and procedure at the top of the meeting.

_____ 4. Gather documentation to plan the terms of the negotiation.

_____ 5. Try to remain flexible when handling conflict.

2. The negotiator and key terms

NOUNS

advantage
basis
commission
concession
condition
counterpart
delivery
emphasis
exclusivity
jurisdiction
labor union
legal issue
license
management
obstacle
opponent
parameter
penalty
rapport
sector
settlement
tactic
warranty

VERBS

compromise
establish
haggle
identify
lose
lose face
maneuver
overcome
win

ADJECTIVES

articulate   tempting
aware   tenacious
beneficial   tentative
charismatic
competent
delicate
fallback
independent
introductory
lasting
persuasive
preliminary
rational

Types of negotiation

Broadly speaking, one can identify three main types of negotiation: **1.** The **win-win** format: two **parties** try to find a **mutually beneficial agreement** and **establish the basis for a lasting** relationship. **2.** Both **teams** look more for **independent advantage** with less emphasis on a **long-term** relationship. **3.** The **win-lose** format: when the two sides see their **counterparts** as opponents, for example in some labor union and management negotiations.

persuasive
polite
rational
firm
flexible
sensitive
confident
clear
competent

knowledgeable about
business sector
culturally aware
constructive
controlled
charismatic
articulate
prepared
honest
tenacious

Negotiating parameters

discount
payment terms
quantity
documentation
delivery
credit
commission
exclusivity
licenses
warranties and guarantees
insurance
quality control
penalties
legal issues and jurisdiction

The negotiation

After initial **small talk** to establish a **good rapport**, both groups normally present their **opening** position. However, **strategies** and **tactics** have been prepared and there is usually **room to maneuver**. Parties will prepare an **ideal position** but will be prepared **to make concessions** and move to a **fallback position** to meet the required **conditions**. **Proposals** and **counter-proposals** will be made as part of this process. It may also be necessary to **identify** and **overcome obstacles** to a settlement. After a great deal of **bargaining** or **haggling**, both parties should **compromise** without **losing face**. Finally, a **deal will be reached** and a **contract will be signed**.

to make
to propose
to consider
to accept
to reject
to appreciate
to agree to
to withdraw

An offer

attractive
reasonable
fair
tempting
tentative
balanced
introductory

to enter into
to conduct
to renew
to resume
to adjourn
to break off

A negotiation

delicate
tough
detailed
preliminary
high-level
marathon
lengthy

> OK. First, perhaps we should start by deciding who has the swivel chair.

Define the parameters of the negotiation.

Prepositions

To negotiate **with** someone
To negotiate **about** something
To negotiate **from** a position of strength
To negotiate **in** good faith

Fill in the blanks. Listen and check.

confident	settlement	haggle	established

Linda: Has our company had a long-term relationship with the other party?

Bob: Our history together goes back several years. In any case, I fully expect these negotiations to turn out as a win-win _____. That company is small and depends on commission from us, and we also get a good discount on orders.

Linda: You seem pretty _____ the negotiations will go well.

Bob: I'm sure we can come up with a mutually beneficial agreement.

Linda: Has management _____ any conditions for you to meet?

Bob: I have the basis for a contract outlined, but management did leave me some room to make concessions in case I need to _____ in the deal.

V O C A B U L A R Y

Match the words with similar meanings.

1. articulate   **a.** charming
2. charismatic   **b.** first
3. preliminary   **c.** logical
4. rational   **d.** stubborn
5. tenacious   **e.** well-spoken

P R A C T I C E

Mark which of the following actions show progress in a negotiation.

	PROGRESS	NO PROGRESS
1. one party accepts a counter-proposal	( )	( )
2. both parties try to compromise	( )	( )
3. one party refuses to haggle	( )	( )
4. two parties overcome an obstacle	( )	( )
5. one party withdraws a proposal	( )	( )

3. Opening – creating the right climate

Vocabulary

NOUNS
climate
colleague
discussion
offer
spare time

VERBS
begin
echo
get down to business
get started
look after
take over

ADJECTIVES
abroad
delighted
follow-up
full
in charge of
polite
positive

At the beginning of a negotiation it is vital to establish:
1. a good relationship with the other party
2. a positive climate in which the discussions can take place.

Greetings

First meeting — How do you do? / Pleased to meet you.

Follow-up meeting — How are you? / Fine. It's good to see you again.

Welcoming — On behalf of..., I'm very glad to welcome you to ..../It's a pleasure to see you here. / We are delighted to be here.

Names

I'm ....
My name is ....
Please call me ....

Introductions

Let me introduce you to ....
This is ....
    he's in charge of ....
    he looks after ....
    he's our ... Director/Manager
    she's just taken over as Head of ....
Have you met ....? I think you've met ....

Small talk

How was your flight?
How was the trip?
Where are you staying?
This isn't your first visit to .... is it?
How was your weekend?

Polite offers

Let me take your coats.
Would you like some coffee?
Should I have a taxi come at
    the end of the meeting?

Getting started

Well, perhaps we should begin.
As we're a little short of time,
    we should get started.
We've got a very full agenda,
    so let's get down to business.

The right climate — a checklist

1. Welcome
2. Greet the visitor
3. Introduce yourselves and colleagues
4. Small talk – ask about their trip
5. Polite offers – a drink
6. Get down to business

Interactive small talk strategies

Show interest – make noises
Really/That's interesting/
    Yes – Yeah I see/Uh-huh

Echo interesting facts
Responsible for three thousand people?
Born in Egypt!?

Answer questions and develop answers
That's right. And ....
Yes. Especially ....

Comment
So, I suppose that you don't have a lot of
    spare time?
So, you have to work abroad a lot?

Take turns – return questions
And you? Do you ski?
What about you? Are you a golfer?

Find common areas
I like ....   – Me too./So do I.
I don't like a .... – Neither do I!/Me, neither!
I think ....   – Absolutely. I agree.

🎞 http://access.englishcentral.com/compass/negotiatingcreatingtherightclimate

Fill in the blanks. Listen and check.

took over	full	offer	colleague

Bob: Good afternoon, Roger. It's nice to see you again. Allow me to introduce Linda Strait, a _____ of mine. She'll be sitting in on our negotiations.

Roger: Delighted to meet you, Linda.

Linda: Likewise. Can I _____ you some coffee or tea, Roger?

Roger: No, thanks. I'm fine. So, Bob, I heard William _____ as head of personnel here at your company.

Bob: That's right. William left sales, so now I'm in charge of these contract negotiations. Since we've got a _____ agenda today, should we get started?

Ⓥ Ⓞ Ⓒ Ⓐ Ⓑ Ⓤ Ⓛ Ⓐ Ⓡ Ⓨ

What is the person doing? Label each sentence or questions using the words below.

greeting	introducing	offering	using small talk	welcoming

1. Is this your first time to visit Florida? _____

2. It's a pleasure to meet you. _____

3. Let me get you some coffee. _____

4. On behalf of Tech Inc., I'd like to welcome you to our office. _____

5. This is Tina Simmons. She's in charge of marketing. _____

Ⓟ Ⓡ Ⓐ Ⓒ Ⓣ Ⓘ Ⓒ Ⓔ

How would you respond? Write a sentence or question using the prompt.

1. I just returned from a business trip to Russia.

   (show interest) _____

2. The temperature in Moscow was ten degrees below zero!

   (echo) _____

3. Have you ever traveled abroad on business?

   (answer and develop) _____

4. Do you like cold weather?

   (answer and return question) _____

5. I prefer warmer climates.

   (answer showing preference in common) _____

4. Agreeing on an agenda

Vocabulary

NOUNS
agenda
host company
length
participant
position
procedure
role
session

VERBS
achieve
aim
assume
concentrate on
draw up
establish
expect
handle
impose
move on
outline
require
run through
sit in
sound
state
suggest
take a break
take minutes

ADJECTIVES
doing for time
formal
global
informal

ADVERBS
at this point

The agenda
While informal negotiations often don't require a more formal agenda, it is usually important to negotiate a procedure and agenda at the start of a meeting. Certainly, an agenda should not be imposed or assumed. As regards chairing or controlling, this is usually the responsibility of the host company.

Procedure
To begin, I think we should first agree on a procedure for the negotiation.
May I suggest that we begin by establishing a procedure for the session?
I think we could begin by outlining our position. Then ....
After that we should hear your presentation.
Then we'll have a question and answer session. Finally ....

Checking for agreement/approval
How does that sound?
Is that okay?
Would you agree?

Global objectives
OK. We're here today to ....
The main objective/purpose of today's meeting is ....
I'd like to start by saying a few words about the meeting today and what we expect to achieve ....

> **Checklist:**
> **Organizing the process**
> 1. Establish a procedure
> 2. Check for agreement
> 3. State global objectives
> 4. Introduce and agree on agenda
> 5. Clarify participants and roles
> 6. Agree on length of meeting
> 7. Handle any questions
> 8. Move to opening statement of positions

Introducing the agenda
We've drawn up an agenda.
Let's just run through the agenda.
As you can see, there are 2/3/4 items on the agenda.
I'd like to take ... first.
We aim to deal with / cover ... under item 3.
We've put ... last.

Negotiating the agenda
We see three issues ....
Can we concentrate on ...?
We would like to look at ....
We would want to consider ....
May we leave that till later and ....

Roles
... is going to sit in.
... is going to take the minutes.
... would like to say a few words about ....
... you're going to give us a presentation.

Length of meeting
It will take two hours. / It won't take long.
I need to be away by .... o'clock. That gives us two hours.
I suggest that we take a break / lunch at ....
How are you doing for time? [Informal context]

Questions
OK. Are there any questions at this point?
Would you like to ask or add anything?
If you have nothing to add, we can move on to outlining our position.

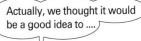

Negotiate the agenda!

Specify length of meeting.

D I A L O G http://access.englishcentral.com/compass/negotiatingagreeingonagenda

Fill in the blanks. Listen and check.

drawn up	sitting in	at this point	concentrate on

Bob: May I suggest the procedure for today's meeting?
Roger: Certainly.
Bob: I assume you've brought the outline for the contract terms your company prefers. Of course, we've _____ some contract terms of our own. So after we both run through the proposals, we can _____ the areas that don't agree. Does that sound alright with you?
Roger: That sounds fine.
Bob: Since Linda is _____ on our negotiations, I've also asked her to take minutes for us. So, _____, I think we're ready to hear the new contract terms.

V O C A B U L A R Y

Match each question with the appropriate response.

1. Do you expect to achieve all of that today?
2. How are we doing for time?
3. Should we move on?
4. How does that sound?
5. May I suggest we first establish the agenda?

a. Yes, if possible.
b. OK. Where should we start?
c. That sounds fine.
d. We have less than an hour left.
e. Not yet. I still want to discuss something.

P R A C T I C E

Choose the best word to complete the sentence.

1. Everyone is _____ to attend a training workshop once a year.
   a. handled   b. imposed   c. required   d. stated

2. Several of the _____ were late because of the weather.
   a. lengths   b. participants   c. roles   d. sessions

3. This is not a problem only in our country. It is a _____ problem.
   a. formal   b. global   c. informal   d. negotiation

4. We _____ to reach our goal before the project's deadline.
   a. aim   b. outline   c. sound   d. achieve

5. You made your company's _____ very clear in your opening statement.
   a. agenda   b. length   c. position   d. session

5. Opening statements – stating your position

NOUNS
activity
brochure
feedback
offer
opportunity
priority
profile
proposal

VERBS
hear from
hold back
interrupt
maneuver
stress

ADJECTIVES
essential
important
in contact
inclusive
less
major
unclear

ADVERBS
accordingly
basically
chiefly
currently
extremely
frequently
immediately

Strategy

1. Holding back – it's important to give yourself some room to maneuver later. So don't present your best offer immediately.
2. Getting feedback – make sure when presenting that you check frequently that the audience follows and has an opportunity to ask questions and comment.

Background to the negotiation

Things began in ... and we have been in contact now for ....
You've all seen our brochures / proposal / offer.
I think you've all had a chance to read our ....
Has anything changed since ...?

Company profile

As you know, the company was established in ....
Our main activity is ....
Our major markets are ....
Currently we ....

Link to position statement

OK. Let me now turn to ....
All right. I should now move on to ....

Inviting interruptions

Let's deal with any questions immediately.
Just interrupt if anything is unclear.
We'll take questions at the end, if that's OK with you.

Stating your position

General
Basically, we are interested in ....
In the long term, we would like to increase ....
We believe it is time for us to develop ....
We are looking for ....

Focus
It is essential for us to ....
... is extremely important for us.
I should stress that ....

Additional
... is a lower priority.
... is less important at the moment.

Invite a response

Are there any questions at this point?
Do you have any comments to make on that?
Would you like to clarify anything?

Your turn

OK. Perhaps we can hear from your side now.
Now I think we can move on to hear your presentation.

Mr. White will now tell us something about the engineering side of the business.

Developing Arguments

Addition
furthermore, moreover, in addition, besides this

Contrast
nevertheless, however, despite this

Highlight
in particular, especially, chiefly, mainly

Cause
therefore, as a result, hence, accordingly

Note:
Use of "we / let's" rather than "I / you."
Where possible, it's more inclusive to say "We'd like to ... " or "Let's start by talking about." Certainly if you are a member of a team, use "we" rather than "I."

D I A L O G http://access.englishcentral.com/compass/negotiatingstatingposition

Fill in the blanks. Listen and check.

stress	profile	priority	brochures

Roger: I don't know if Linda is aware of our company _____, but basically our company's major interest is in paper products.

Linda: I did have the opportunity to learn a little about your company before this meeting. Bob showed me one of your company's _____.

Roger: Great! Well, currently the situation between our companies has been extremely beneficial for both parties. And I want to _____ that our company hopes to continue such a relationship.

Bob: I'm happy to hear that, Roger. That's also a _____ on our side.

V O C A B U L A R Y

Find an adverb in the Vocabulary list with a similar meaning and write it in the blank.

1. because of that _____

2. at this time _____

3. mainly _____

4. often _____

5. right away _____

P R A C T I C E

If the phrases mean the same, circle the "=" sign. If they are opposites, cross it out.

EX: nice ⊜ kind   black ✖ white

1. Feel free to interrupt any time. = Hold your questions until the end.

2. I don't have any questions at this point. = Everything is clear so far.

3. It is essential. = It's not important.

4. This is not a high priority. = All other points are less important.

5. It's our main activity. = It's the major focus of our business.

6. Clarifying positions

Vocabulary

NOUNS
argument
consideration
factor
figure
issue
opportunity
position
priority

VERBS
clarify
depend on
discuss
go ahead
guarantee
have in mind
ignore
look at
mean
move on
paraphrase
require
respect
respond
signal
summarize
take into account
value

ADJECTIVES
accurate
effective
further
main
major
minimum
secondary
sympathetic

ADVERBS
approximately

Listening

To guarantee the full understanding, an effective listener will use different techniques:

- asking questions
- paraphrasing others' arguments
- summarizing positions constantly

Advantages of listening well

1. Understand the other party's negotiating position
2. Develop arguments that respond to their needs
3. Show that you are sympathetic to their position
4. Signal that you respect/value what they have to say

Confirming negotiating positions	Responding
So, you ... Is that an accurate summary of where you stand? So, for you, this is an opportunity to .... The most important thing for you is .... As I understand it, you would like to .... Is that right?	That's right. Exactly. Yes, it is. Not exactly, I said ....

Asking for clarification	Clarifying
I didn't understand. What exactly do you mean by ...? Could you clarify one point for me? When you say ... are you saying that ...? Could you say a little bit more about	When I said ... I meant .... Perhaps I should clarify that. Of course. Not exactly. What I was saying was .... Sure.

General questions	Encouraging/showing interest
Can I just ask you a question about .... I'd be interested to know more about .... Could you tell us something about ...? Could I move on to another question?	Go ahead. Of course. Yes, certainly. Please do. Go ahead.

Defining priorities
Is ... your main consideration?
How important is ... to you?
... is of secondary importance?

Direct answer
It is our major priority.
It is a secondary issue.
It is not a main consideration.

Indirect answer
Well, we need to discuss this further.
It is something we need to take into account.
It is not something we can ignore.

Getting the facts straight
Can you give me an idea of how much/many ...?
Approximately, what figure did you have in mind for ...?
How soon ...?
What ... terms would you be expecting?
What would be the minimum ... you would consider?

Direct answer
We would require a delivery date before January.
We are looking at a figure of 3,000.
Around three million dollars.

Indirect answer
It's difficult to say at this moment.
I can't really answer that at the moment.
That depends on various factors.

D I A L O G http://access.englishcentral.com/compass/negotiatingclarifyingpositions

Fill in the blanks. Listen and check.

secondary	sympathetic	require	minimum

Bob: So, if I may summarize your company's position, the new contract would _____ us to guarantee a higher annual order.

Roger: That's right. As you can see from the figure we've calculated, in order to deliver at the current discount rate, we need a _____ order of 10,000 units.

Bob: Of course we are _____ to the position your company is in. However, there are certain factors needing consideration on our end as well. For example, we have to take into account the growth we expect in sales next year. The greater cost of the order is really of _____ importance to us.

V O C A B U L A R Y

Correct the error in each of the following sentences.

1. If I understand correctly, we are looking to a final total of around $50,000.

2. None of us took to account how long the negotiation would take.

3. Now that we agree on that point, we can move up to the next item on the agenda.

4. Our agreement to the contract depends of three important factors.

5. We had on mind a slight hire figure for the contract.

P R A C T I C E

Put the following statements and questions in logical order (1=first, 5=last).

_____ **Woman:** Are the figures listed in this table accurate for last year?

_____ **Man:** No, the figures are averaged over the past five years.

_____ **Woman:** Before we move on, can I ask a question?

_____ **Man:** Sure. Go ahead.

_____ **Woman:** I see. Thank you.

7. Making and responding to proposals

Vocabulary

NOUNS
advantage
direction
parameters
phase
point of view
process
proposal
relationship
review
scenario

VERBS
accept
agree
develop
go along with
propose
respond
see
set
show one's hand
sound
take time

ADJECTIVES
alternative
certain
concrete
preferred
prepared

ADVERBS
essentially
generally
importantly
initially
negatively
ultimately

Summarizing

Before moving on to concrete proposals, it is sometimes useful to take time to summarize.

Introducing a review

So, it seems that there are several ways that we could work together.
I think we could develop our relationship in various ways.
Perhaps we could take time to think generally about ....

Your view on things

From our point of view,...
For our company,...
As we see it, you want ....

Checking

Is that how you see it?
Did you have other ideas?
How does that sound?

> **Redefining objectives**
> Initially,...
> At the outset ....
> During the first phase,...
> In the short – medium – long term,...
> Essentially,...
> Ultimately,...
> Basically,...
> Most importantly,...

Concrete proposals

The supplier will usually start this process. The advantage is then given to the customer who doesn't have to show his hand until he first hears what the supplier is proposing. On the other hand, making a proposal first may set the parameters for discussion and it could be an advantage if you want the negotiation to go in a certain direction.

Starting proposals

We are now ready to move on to more concrete proposals.
OK. I think we can now begin responding to your proposals.

Making proposals

We propose ....
Our proposal is to ....
We could offer you ....
We suggest ....
We are prepared to ....
How / What about ...?

Don't react too negatively to first proposals!

Counter-proposals

From our point of view, we would rather have ....
Could we offer an alternative proposal?
Our preferred scenario would be ....
Supposing we ....
How about if we ....

Reacting to proposals

Positively	Neutrally	Negatively
That sounds fine. I think we can go along with that.	We might be able to do that. I see what you're saying. I understand why you think so.	That could be a problem. We couldn't agree to that. I'm afraid that we can't accept that.

Fill in the blanks. Listen and check.

respond	point of view	propose	alternative

Roger: Let me see if I have this correct. From your _____, it's more important to order the units you need rather than to get the cheapest price.

Bob: Right. Most importantly, we don't want to keep a lot of back stock. And we're prepared to suffer a slight increase in cost for orders if necessary.

Roger: Then may I suggest an _____ proposal. With your past orders ranging between 600 and 800 units, I would _____ setting the discount rate 3% lower. Would you be willing to accept that?

Bob: Before I _____ to that offer, let me do a few calculations of my own.

V O C A B U L A R Y

Mark each response as positive, negative, or neutral.

	POSITIVE	NEUTRAL	NEGATIVE
1. We're ready to accept such a deal.	( )	( )	( )
2. I don't think the offer is to our advantage.	( )	( )	( )
3. It's an interesting proposal.	( )	( )	( )
4. That sounds reasonable.	( )	( )	( )
5. We'll need to take time to consider the offer.	( )	( )	( )

P R A C T I C E

Choose the word with a similar meaning as the underlined words.

1. At first, the offer sounded very good, but as we learned more it was not good.

   a. Essentially   b. Initially   c. Negatively   d. Ultimately

2. In negotiations, as well as in poker, you don't want to show your cards too early.

   a. direction   b. hand   c. phase   d. scenario

3. Let's go over the terms of the contract one more time.

   a. phases   b. processes   c. parameters   d. reviews

4. They finally accepted our proposal with only a few changes.

   a. generally   b. importantly   c. initially   d. ultimately

5. We can go along with your proposal.

   a. agree with   b. respond to   c. see about   d. take time

8. Bargaining

NOUNS
acceptance
approval
authority
deal
improvement
objective
proviso
requirement
stage

VERBS
consider
get back to
go along with
guarantee
link to
reduce
refer back
refuse
reiterate
reject
stress
take into account
undertake

ADJECTIVES
acceptable
basic
willing

At the bargaining stage, the acceptance of offers is linked to conditions.

Restating your position

Let me just clarify our basic position.
Perhaps I should reiterate our objective here.
Can I just stress that ....

But we would want a guarantee of no rain!

BUY YOUR DREAM HOME IN ENGLAND

Setting conditions.

Setting conditions

| We might be willing to ....
That's acceptable ....
We can agree to ....
That's fine ....
We could offer you ....
We might consider ....
What would you say if we offered you ....
We could be willing to/ happy to .... | **if
provided that
on condition that
so long as
providing
with the proviso that
when** | you can ....

you guarantee ....

you reduce ....

you undertake .... |

Responding in the bargaining phase

Accepting
That is acceptable. • OK. We can agree to that. • I think we could go along with that now.

Refuse with new offer
We couldn't agree to that but we could .... • That would be difficult. However, would you consider ...? • I'm afraid this is not acceptable. But why not ...?

Accept with a condition
That's fine if you .... • If you ... then we have a deal. • Provided that you ..., then we can agree.

Reject
I'm afraid that wouldn't meet our requirements. • Even with this offer, we couldn't accept. • Despite ..., we can't agree to this.

Authority problem
I'm afraid I don't have the authority to give approval on that. • I'll have to get back to you on that. • I would need to refer back on that.

Linking words

refusing	accepting
Despite this offer, we	Owing to ..., we will ....
In spite of this improvement,...	Following your new offer of ..., we find that ....
Even with this new offer, we	Taking ... into account, we can now ....
Despite the fact that you have	As you have reduced ..., we will ....
In spite of the fact that you have	Since you have increased ..., we can ....
Although you have	You have .... Therefore we will ....

D I A L O G http://access.englishcentral.com/compass/negotiatingbargaining

Fill in the blanks. Listen and check.

deal	proviso	reiterate	acceptable

Roger: Let me _____, if you guarantee a minimum order the discount is higher.

Bob: We understand, but we have to consider realistic expectations of our market. What would be the minimum _____ order to receive an 8.5% discount on the total order?

Roger: We'd be willing to offer that kind of discount with the _____ that your company guaranteed an order of 800 units.

Bob: I think our company could go along with that.

Roger: Then, do we have a _____?

V O C A B U L A R Y

Match the words with similar meanings.

1. guarantee   **a.** consider

2. reduce   **b.** lower

3. refuse   **c.** promise

4. take into account   **d.** reject

5. undertake   **e.** try

P R A C T I C E

What kind of bargaining is used? Label each statement using the words below.

accepting	making new offer	setting condition	rejecting

1. Our company is willing to go along with that. _____

2. Those requirements are too strict for us. _____

3. Provided that we get this amount for two years, it's fine. _____

4. So long as you order 100 units, we've got a deal. _____

5. That's impossible. But would you consider another price? _____

9. Handling conflict and resolving sticking points

Vocabulary

NOUNS

commitment
common ground
compromise
concession
intonation
mediator
objection
obstacle
personality
sticking point
tone

VERBS

achieve
adjourn
call it a day
come back to
cool down
encounter
get in the way
give ground
keep sight of
overcome
preface
put one's mind at rest
reassure
resolve
reveal
take a look at
terminate
threaten

ADJECTIVES

achievable
confrontational
demanding
fresh
mutual
potential
reasonable
sensitive
unable
underlying
unrealistic

ADVERBS

fully
seriously

Most negotiations will encounter difficult problems. There is a much greater chance that solutions will be found if both parties keep sight of the main objectives and maintain a positive tone.

Always stress the positive

I think we should look again at where we have agreement.
I think we should take a quick look at what we have achieved so far.
There is no problem in relation to ....
As far as ... is concerned, we agree.

Identifying obstacles

The major obstacle at the moment seems to be ....
The main sticking point here is ....
... is getting in the way of an agreement.

Analyzing an obstacle

Let's look at this in a little more detail.
What is the underlying problem here?
What exactly are your objections to ...?

Creating solutions

I think we both need to give a little ground here.
What do you think is a reasonable solution?
A compromise could be to ....

Reassuring

Let me reassure you that ....
Let me put your mind at rest about ....
Don't worry about ....

Postponing

I think it would be a good idea to come back to this later.
Perhaps we should adjourn to reconsider.
Let's break and hopefully we can come back with some fresh ideas.

Asking and showing understanding

I hope you can appreciate our difficulties with this.
I realize that this is difficult.
I fully understand ....

Threatening

If you are unable to move on this, we will have to ....
I'm afraid we'll have to call it a day unless ....
If you can't offer us something, we'll have to look elsewhere.

Terminate the negotiation

I think we have gone as far as we can today.
I'm afraid that we're not going to reach agreement today.
I think we should both seriously reconsider our positions.

Causes of conflict
Unrealistic demands
Personality differences
Poor communication
Misunderstanding
Failure to appreciate cultural difference
Lack of commitment

Conflict resolution strategies
Identify obstacles and overcome them
Set achievable goals
Be sensitive to others
Respect cultural difference
Summarize and stress common ground
Stress mutual interest in making a deal
Change your package
Make concessions
Take time out to think and cool down
Leave and return later to problem areas
Change personnel/location
Involve a mediator
Forget it and call it a day!

Conflict is not always negative!
Potential benefits:
Moves the negotiation forward quickly.
Reveals differences which need to be resolved.
Improves understanding of positions.

Language style:
You can appear less confrontational with a few simple techniques:
1. Moderate your requests with "perhaps" or "maybe" to sound less demanding.
2. Use modal verbs *could, would, may, might.*
3. Preface disagreement with "I'm afraid ...." or "I'm sorry ...."

Note: Intonation
The way you say things also matters! Intonation can play a very important role in creating a positive atmosphere.

DIALOG http://access.englishcentral.com/compass/negotiatinghandlingconflictresolvingsticki

Fill in the blanks. Listen and check.

obstacles	overcome	demands	common ground

Bob: Let's take a look at the terms of the rest of the contract. I want to make sure there are no other sticking points.

Roger: Now that we've found _____ on the annual order of minimum units, I can't think of any other potential problems we would need to _____.

Bob: What about this clause about your company's responsibility in the case of failure to deliver orders on time?

Roger: I'm willing to negotiate that clause as long as your _____ aren't unrealistic.

Bob: Once we achieve agreement on this clause, I think all of the _____ will be resolved.

VOCABULARY

Circle the word that does not belong in each group.

1. achievable   doable   possible   unable
2. agreement   compromise   concession   objection
3. adjourn   call it a day   encounter   terminate
4. fresh   mutual   new   original
5. detail   mediator   party   witness

PRACTICE

Write the words with a similar meaning as the underlined words.

come back	cool down	maintained	reassure you	requested

1. Let me <u>put your mind at rest</u>. We guarantee delivery in two days. _____
2. Now I want to <u>return</u> to the problem of returning over-stock. _____
3. One of the parties <u>asked for</u> a second meeting the following week. _____
4. The supplier <u>kept</u> the initial price throughout the negotiation. _____
5. We should take a break to give both sides time to <u>calm down</u>. _____

10. Closing a negotiation

Vocabulary

NOUNS
agreement
basis
direction
exclusivity
front
loose end
progress
step

VERBS
agree on
award
breach
circulate
cover
depart
draft
draw up
enter into
go over
honor
put together
ratify
reflect
resolve
run over
sign
suit
tie up

ADJECTIVES
accurate
binding
detailed
exclusive
legal
oral
outstanding
partial
right
unresolved
valid
verbal

Closing signals

OK, perhaps we should stop at this point.
So, that brings us to the end of ....
Right. I think that covers everything for today.

Progress made

We've made some / good / excellent progress.
We've taken a step in the right direction.
We didn't get as far as we hoped but ....

Summarize

Can I just run over the main points?
Let's go over the main points again.

Review areas of agreement

On the ... front, we agreed ....
As far as ... is concerned, we agreed ....
We've agreed on the following ....

State unresolved areas

There's still the question of ... to resolve.
Outstanding issues are ....
We can tie up the loose ends at a later date.

Checking and confirming

Do you agree with that?
Does that reflect what we said?
Is that an accurate summary?

Action points for the future

We'll review this again in six months.
Would you like that in writing?
We'll put together a written proposal.
We will draw up a final contract.
We'll circulate the minutes ....
Pete's been keeping notes.
We'll let you have a detailed summary.

Next meeting

Could you make ...?
Should we say 4 o'clock? Does that suit you?
I suggest we meet at the same time next week.

Positive close

I think we've both got a good deal.
It remains for me to thank you for coming and ....
That was a very positive start.
I hope it's the basis for a long-term relationship.
We can finish there. I look forward to our next meeting.

Closing checklist

Confirm that you have an agreement
Signal the end of the meeting
Refer to progress
Summarize areas of agreement
State unresolved areas
Check understanding
Outline action points for the future
Set the next meeting
Depart on a positive note

A CONTRACT

binding	To break	To draft
exclusive	To breach	To draw up
verbal	To cancel	To ratify
legal	To conclude	To award
valid	To sign	To honor
oral	To enter into	
written		

OK. I think we have an agreement.

We have reached an agreement.

We have a deal.

Could you just clarify what you mean by 'partial exclusivity'?

Check if something is not clear!

Ⓓ Ⓘ Ⓐ Ⓛ Ⓞ Ⓖ http://access.englishcentral.com/compass/closingnegotiation

Fill in the blanks. Listen and check.

suits	agreement	legal	go over

Roger: I think that ties up all the loose ends with the contract.

Bob: After your company draws up the final contract based on the new terms we've agreed on, I'll have my superiors _____ it before we officially ratify it.

Roger: Of course. And it's probably a good idea to have the _____ departments of both sides run over the contract again.

Bob: I was a bit surprised at how fast we made progress to reach a final _____.

Roger: That just reflects the type of relationship our companies have.

Bob: I think we've put together a good deal that _____ both sides.

Ⓥ Ⓞ Ⓒ Ⓐ Ⓑ Ⓤ Ⓛ Ⓐ Ⓡ Ⓨ

Match the two parts to make complete sentences.

1. The supplier breached ...   **a.** a memo to remind us about the meeting.
2. Both parties departed ...   **b.** the agreement so the contract was void.
3. The government awarded ...   **c.** the deal before he read the small print.
4. She circulated ...   **d.** the contract to the company.
5. The manager signed ...   **e.** the meeting happy with the progress.

Ⓟ Ⓡ Ⓐ Ⓒ Ⓣ Ⓘ Ⓒ Ⓔ

Circle the best word to complete the sentence.

1. It took them over three hours to _____ all the loose ends with the contract.
   a. draft   b. put together   c. sign   d. tie up

2. The contract is legally _____ because both parties signed it.
   a. binding   b. detailed   c. oral   d. partial

3. There are few _____ issues left to resolve before the negotiations are completed.
   a. accurate   b. exclusive   c. outstanding   d. right

4. We made a _____ agreement over the phone regarding the price.
   a. legal   b. right   c. unresolved   d. verbal

5. Our agreement should become the _____ for a good working relationship between our companies.
   a. basis   b. exclusivity   c. front   d. step

11. Negotiating – an overview

Vocabulary

NOUNS
agenda
background
basis
contract
deal
factor
length
objective
obstacle
point of view
position
progress
role

VERBS
agree
clarify
depend on
draw up
get started
hear from
interrupt
look forward to
meet
move on
outline
remain
review
run over
sound
turn to

ADJECTIVES
essential
major
reasonable
willing

ADVERBS
basically
correctly

Opening

Welcome to .... It's good to see you. ➤ I think you have met ... ➤ So, how was your trip? ➤ Can I get you something to drink? ➤ OK. Should we get started? ➤ To begin, we should agree on an agenda. ➤ May I suggest that we ... OK? ➤ Just to clarify roles .... ➤ As for the length of meeting, I hope we can finish by .... ➤ If you have nothing to add, we can move on to outlining our position.

First moves

The main objective of today's meeting is to .... ➤ To begin, I would like to review the background up to today. ➤ OK. Let me now turn to our objectives today in more detail. ➤ Just interrupt me if you want to clarify anything. ➤ Basically, we would like to .... It is essential for us to .... ➤ Furthermore .... In addition .... ➤ How does that sound? Any questions? ➤ OK. Can we now hear from your side?

Questions

Could we just clarify one thing?

How important to you is ...?

So, if I understand you correctly, you would like ....

Sure. Of course.

That depends on several factors.

Yes, although let me clarify one thing ....

Bargaining

We propose...

We would be willing to ... if ....

That is out of the question.

What do you think is reasonable?

We can agree to that.

OK. From our point of view....

I think we could go along with that provided that ....

The major obstacle seems to be ....

Well, so long as you .... then we could ....

Great. I think we are making progress.

Agreement and Close

I think we have a deal! ➤ Can I just run over the main points of the agreement? ➤ We have agreed to .... We will .... at a later date. ➤ Is that correct? Do you agree? ➤ OK. We can draw up a contract next week. ➤ It just remains for me to say thank you for coming. ➤ I think we have a good deal and the basis for a long relationship. ➤ I look forward to our next meeting. ➤ For now, we can finish here.

⬛ http://access.englishcentral.com/compass/negotiatinganoverview

Fill in the blanks. Listen and check.

basis	factor	got started	background

Bob: Do you have any observations about how the negotiations went?

Linda: Well, I didn't have much _____ about past negotiations with the company, but on the _____ of my experience, it went very well.

Bob: I didn't anticipate any major obstacles going into the negotiations. We've always managed to make good deals with them in the past.

Linda: From my point of view, it seemed both sides were willing to bargain from the outset. And another _____ that helped make quick progress was outlining each party's ideal terms as the meeting _____.

ⓋⓄⒸⒶⒷⓊⓁⒶⓇⓎ

Fill in the blanks to complete the definitions.

clarify	major	objective	reasonable	remains

1. A big or important point is a _____ point.

2. If you want someone to explain in detail, you want them to _____.

3. The thing you are trying to achieve is your _____.

4. A condition that is OK or acceptable is _____.

5. When something still has yet to be done, that thing _____ to be done.

ⓅⓇⒶⒸⓉⓘⒸⒺ

Put the following sentences in logical order for a negotiation (1=first, 5=last).

_____ **a.** Everything sounds great! So I think we're ready to draw up a contract.

_____ **b.** Good afternoon, ladies and gentlemen. Welcome to Big Corp.

_____ **c.** I think we're ready to move on to hearing your opening proposal.

_____ **d.** Let's go over the agenda before we do anything else.

_____ **e.** That's a very interesting offer you've made.

12. Phrasal verbs and idioms for negotiating

Vocabulary

VERBS
break a deadlock
break down
build up
carry on
clinch a deal
come down
bog down
give ground
give in
go along
go around in circles
improvise
iron out
keep something up one's
  sleeve
maintain
pin down
play by ear
reach a stalemate
reveal
rush into
show one's hand
stand on
stick to one's guns
work out

ADJECTIVES
anxious
precise

A story of negotiating using 'Phrasal Verbs'

At the beginning of the negotiation the other team asked me where I **stood on** prices. I told them that I had **worked out** some figures regarding discounts and quantity. I said that I expected them to **come down** from $40 per unit to $30. They refused to **be pinned down** too early on a precise price. They explained that they didn't want to **rush into** anything. I was anxious to **build up** a relationship so I decided to **carry on**. I was hoping that we could **iron out** any difficulties as we **went along**. However, the negotiation eventually **broke down** when the other team refused to **give in** on price and **come down** to our asking price.

Phrasal Verbs

To work something out (= to calculate)
To rush into (= to move forward too quickly)
To build up (= to expand and develop)
To carry on (= to continue)
To stand on (= to have an opinion/position on)
To come down (= to reduce a bargaining position)
To pin someone down (= to get their precise thoughts about)

To give in (= to concede)
To go along (= to proceed)
To break down (= to fail)
To iron out (= to remove)

Idioms – strategy

Keep your cards close to your chest. = Don't reveal your position.

Don't show your hand yet. = Don't reveal your position.

Keep something up your sleeve! = Hold bargaining points back for later in the negotiation.

Let's play it by ear. = Listen and improvise accordingly.

Stick to your guns! = Maintain your position.

Idioms – progress

We're going round in circles. = Repeat without making progress.

We both need to give a little ground here. = Make concessions.

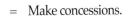

We're getting bogged down. = Focusing too much on one thing and not making progress.

We have reached a stalemate. = Arrived at a position where progress and concessions have stopped.

We broke the deadlock. = Moved past a major sticking point.

We clinched a deal. = Reached agreement

Fill in the blanks. Listen and check.

give ground	worked out	up my sleeve	bogged down

Linda: If the company had stood on their minimum order or their discount, it would have _____ the negotiations.

Bob: Thankfully, they were willing to come down from the original 10,000 units.

Linda: You also had to _____ in accepting a smaller discount in the end.

Bob: Actually, I am quite pleased the way things _____. The discount price we got is better than the discount our boss told me to accept. But I kept our boss' suggested discount price _____. When Roger offered a better discount, it clinched the deal.

ⓋⓄⒸⒶⒷⓊⓁⒶⓇⓎ

Match the phrasal verb or idiom with the correct picture.

a.

b.

c.

1. break down

2. build up

3. go around in circles

4. iron out

5. pin down

6. show one's hand

d.

e.

f.

ⓅⓇⒶⒸⓉⒾⒸⒺ

Find a verb in the Vocabulary list with a similar meaning. Write it in the blank.

1. to act without practice or rehearsal - _____

2. to continue or keep without changing - _____

3. to go to a point that is impossible to move beyond - _____

4. to run or move quickly into - _____

5. to surrender or give up - _____

13. Cross-cultural tips

NOUNS

authority
collaboration
competition
consensus
documentation
flexibility
humor
loyalty
negotiator
partnership
preference
preliminaries
proposition
recognition
reflection
reliability
ritual
status
tactic
threat
wit
zone

VERBS

adapt
appreciate
brief
conduct
entertain
equate
exchange
favor
prioritize
save face
socialize

ADJECTIVES

aggressive   impatient
conservative   modest
efficient   strict
enthusiastic   superficial
excessive   volatile
impassive

ADVERBS

extremely

The following is a checklist of points to consider when preparing for international negotiation.

Relationship building

Some cultures view the opening process of relationship building as extremely important.
Some cultures have strict rules regarding the use of names and titles. Know them!
Some cultures appreciate attempts to learn about and take an interest in a country.
Some cultures see the exchange of business cards as an important ritual.
Some cultures value formality over informality. Dress and react accordingly.
Some cultures expect to receive business gifts. Get briefed!
Some cultures equate status and authority. Know who you are talking to.
Some cultures have very specific ways to entertain and socialize. You may have to adapt.

Negotiating strategy

Some cultures favor consensus, collaboration and win-win over aggressive competition.
Some cultures appreciate flexibility over excessive planning.
Some cultures prioritize specific selling propositions: is it technology, needs, price?
Some cultures employ indirect communication styles in preference to straight speaking.
Some cultures use silence to indicate agreement, not hostility.
Some cultures disapprove of pressure tactics.
Some cultures see the negotiation as a place for discussion, not decision.
Some cultures dislike open displays of emotion and feeling.
Some cultures work with a limited bargaining zone.
Some cultures will see the negotiation of contract documentation as central.

The individual

Some cultures conduct negotiations with teams, not with individuals.
Some cultures are changing slowly to recognize women as negotiators.
Some cultures view the company as more important than the individual.
Some cultures value personal connections and contacts in business and society.

Time

Some cultures value reflection and consensus over speed. Negotiations can take time.
Some cultures look more for longer-term partnerships than others.
Some cultures like to set and respect deadlines.

Some Quick Cross-Cultural Comparisons

Country	Characteristics	Tactics	Key needs
U.S.A.	enthusiastic – open tough – competitive friendly – superficial action oriented – impatient	time pressure bargaining small concessions power – threat	"win" the best deal get results cooperation recognition
Japan	formal – polite group focused impassive efficient – advanced technology	logical show commitment time delays linked package deal	save face long preliminaries long-term relationship gifts
U.K.	verbally indirect polite – formal can seem unprepared fair	good deal for both parties humor and wit conservative presentations fair offer – modest concessions	"win-win" outcome reliability private space progress
Latin countries	emotional – lively personal – volatile enthusiastic	bargaining emotion changes – last minute delays	understanding personal relationship loyalty

D I A L O G http://access.englishcentral.com/compass/negotiatingcrossculturaltips

Fill in the blanks. Listen and check.

tactics	proposition	adapt	briefed

Bob: Next week, I'll be one of the negotiators involved in ironing out a
_____ to form a partnership with a distributor in Taiwan.

Linda: Do you have much experience in negotiating with Taiwanese businesses?

Bob: Not really. I've been _____ on some aspects of Taiwan's business
culture. Formality is going to be the biggest issue for me in those negotiations.

Linda: It probably won't be too difficult to _____ your normal negotiating
_____. No doubt, they have studied American culture and expect you
to employ certain strategies during the negotiations.

V O C A B U L A R Y

Mark the culture probably described by each phrase. More than one answer is possible.

	American	British	Japanese	Latin
1. brings gifts to a meeting	( )	( )	( )	( )
2. does not get down to business right away	( )	( )	( )	( )
3. enjoys a good joke related to the topic	( )	( )	( )	( )
4. keeps asking for lower/higher prices	( )	( )	( )	( )
5. might start shouting in a difficult meeting	( )	( )	( )	( )
6. worries about being late to meetings	( )	( )	( )	( )

P R A C T I C E

Circle the word that best completes the sentence.

1. The _____ for our negotiations is tomorrow!

   a. deadline   b. flexibility   c. loyalty   d. status

2. In some cultures, the _____ greeting is to give a person a kiss on each cheek.

   a. authority   b. humor   c. reflection   d. ritual

3. The group could not reach a _____, so the meeting was a failure.

   a. competition   b. consensus   c. threat   d. zone

4. We could not accept the gifts because the gifts were _____ and made us feel indebted.

   a. aggressive   b. efficient   c. excessive   d. volatile

5. The way she _____ made me believe I had made an extremely rude remark.

   a. entertained   b. favored   c. prioritized   d. reacted

14. Golden rules

Practice and rehearse key English phrases.

NOUNS
assumption
climate
collaboration
confusion
gain
package
perspective
priority
procedure
psychology
rollback
session
target

VERBS
communicate
identify
lock
recheck
reveal
threaten

ADJECTIVES
bogged down
cheap
complex
consistent
global
positive
psychological
sensitive
unrealistic
valuable
whole

ADVERBS
constructively
efficiently
positively
simply

DO
- have clear objectives with strategies for concession and rollback.
- know the negotiating culture of your partner
- agree on roles and tactics for your negotiating team.
- establish a positive climate of collaboration when you meet.
- agree on a procedure at the beginning with targets for each session.
- communicate your objectives simply and efficiently.
- listen to the other side to identify their priorities.
- react positively and constructively to proposals.
- identify common areas and win-win solutions for both parties.
- be flexible and maintain a global perspective on the whole package.
- be sensitive to the psychology of the other party.
- say 'yes' to the person even when you have to say 'no' to the idea.
- when bargaining, give what is cheap to you and valuable to them.
- be consistent.
- avoid misunderstanding and confusion by checking and rechecking.
- respect time and try to move forward efficiently.
- reach agreement.
- summarize the deal.
- define the future relationship.

Negotiators are born, not made.

DON'T
- set unrealistic targets.
- use language which is too complex for people to understand.
- try to employ 'clever' psychological tactics.
- reveal your position too quickly.
- make assumptions about the other party's position.
- say 'no' to a proposal too quickly.
- limit yourself with short-term thinking about short-term gain.
- lock yourself into positions.
- let yourself become bogged down in details.
- threaten the other side.
- stop listening if you disagree.
- make promises you can't keep.
- leave a negotiation without understanding the deal.

I think you will find our price very reasonable.

CLICK!

Don't threaten!

DIALOG

 http://access.englishcentral.com/compass/negotiatinggoldenrules

Fill in the blanks. Listen and check.

sensitive	identified	psychology	package

Bob: It is a good assumption that other cultures know more about our business _____ than we know about theirs.

Linda: Are you worried about confusion when you try to communicate with the representatives from Taiwan in English?

Bob: Of course I should be _____ to the language I use, but I'm sure the company has _____ their best English speakers to send to the negotiations.

Linda: Will this be a preliminary session for the proposed partnership?

Bob: Uh-hu. We're simply going to outline a few ideas. Later we'll work out the details of the whole _____ for the deal.

VOCABULARY

Find the mistake in the definition and correct it using a word from the Vocabulary list.

1. A deal that has many parts and is difficult to understand is simple.

2. If you consider the "big picture", you have a narrow perspective.

3. People who seem agreeable or relaxed have negative personalities.

4. Something that is worth a lot to you is cheap.

5. When someone keeps changing his or her mind or doing things in different ways, the person is not flexible.

PRACTICE

Mark each idea as a good idea (DO) or bad idea (DON'T) for a meeting.

	DO	DON'T
1. try to pressure the other party to win what you want	( )	( )
2. ask more than once to make sure things are clear	( )	( )
3. try to share ideas without talking a long time	( )	( )
4. focus on details to make sure you get everything you want	( )	( )
5. try to understand the other party's mind	( )	( )

CHAPTER 6

Writing For International Business:
E-mails, Letters and Reports

1. Successful writing

NOUNS
abbreviation
conclusion
content
familiarity
feedback
format
gender
grammar
header
jargon
key point
layout
message
objective
opening
phrase
punctuation
sequence
spelling
style
tone

VERBS
amend
bullet
decide
draft
evaluate
link
pay attention to
plan
project
reinforce

ADJECTIVES
concise
courteous
instant
relevant
sexist
specific

ADVERBS
out loud

Effective business writing is essential in today's dynamic environment. Follow the guidelines below to improve your writing.

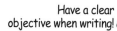

Have a clear objective when writing!

Plan before you write

- establish a clear objective
- plan how much time you will need
- decide what and how much to write
- write to get the answer you want

Know your reader

- include only relevant information
- remain courteous and polite
- adapt style and tone to the reader's
  - specific relationship with you
  - professional position: internal / external / place in hierarchy
  - level of familiarity with topic
  - cultural background
  - age
  - gender (avoid sexist language)

Structure the information clearly

- format with a professional layout
- have a clear opening and conclusion
- plan a logical sequence
- organize your ideas into paragraphs
- link ideas together with connecting words and phrases
- use headers and / or bullet points to highlight key points

Select the right language

- be concise: sentences [15-20 words] – paragraphs [7/8 lines]
- use plain everyday English
- avoid jargon, abbreviations and complex words
- be careful not to repeat words and phrases
- start and finish with the correct phrases
- pay attention to grammar, spelling and punctuation

Finally ... evaluate, amend and send

- give yourself time to review content, format, language and style
- read it out loud to check it sounds natural
- check grammar, punctuation and spelling again
- get feedback from a colleague

The Writing Process

Plan before you write ➤ Consider the reader ➤ Structure the information ➤ Select the right language ➤ Draft, evaluate and amend ➤ Send

Why write? Why not telephone?

People need a written record.
The message is complicated.
Writing can help you to clarify thoughts.
An instant reaction isn't required.
Everyone should get the same message.
Personal authority can be reinforced.
Corporate image can be projected.

When to write?
Make sure your e-mail arrives on Tuesday or Wednesday.

I will deal with it next Monday.

Friday mail will be read on Monday!

K.I.S.S. = Keep It Short + Simple

D I A L O G

Fill in the blanks. Listen and check.

key point	content	concise	pay attention

Linda: Did you see the message posted on the bulletin board, Mark?

Mark: I saw something there this morning, but I didn't _____ to it. Why?

Linda: I just thought it was a strange message. For one thing, I don't think the _____ is relevant to our office. I was also offended by the sexist language.

Mark: What was the topic of the message?

Linda: The _____ was criticizing the company's lack of employee accountability. But the message was several pages long. I didn't read the whole thing.

Mark: Sounds like someone needs to learn how to make their messages more _____.

V O C A B U L A R Y

Circle the word with a similar meaning as the underlined word.

1. He did not know how to <u>fix</u> the mistakes in his writing.

   a. amend   b. bullet   c. plan   d. reinforce

2. I received a very <u>polite</u> letter replying to my complaint.

   a. concise   b. courteous   c. instant   d. specific

3. The report was difficult to understand because the ideas were not <u>connected</u> well.

   a. drafted   b. linked   c. projected   d. reinforced

4. What is your <u>purpose</u> in writing this memo?

   a. feedback   b. format   c. jargon   d. objective

5. You explained everything very clearly in the <u>end</u> of the report.

   a. conclusion   b. gender   c. sequence   d. tone

P R A C T I C E

Put the following items in order according to size (a=smallest, e=largest).

_____ **1.** document

_____ **2.** paragraph

_____ **3.** phrase / clause

_____ **4.** sentence

_____ **5.** word

2. Organizing information

Vocabulary

NOUNS
chronology
conclusion
development
incident
introduction
literature
process
pyramid
report
sequence
technique

VERBS
access
activate
brainstorm
invert
list
prioritize
sort out

ADJECTIVES
classic
concise
general
instructional
practical
promotional
specific

ADVERBS
severely
steadily

Some business writing may be done without much preparation. However, complex information requires planning and organization. Here are some practical techniques you can use!

How to plan

Work in five stages:
1. write down your objective
2. brainstorm possible content
3. prioritize and select information
4. prepare an outline with main points
5. fill in the details and start writing

Outline Report

Impact of e-commerce
1. The manufacturer
   - supply chain savings
   - marketing/pricing
2. The consumer
   - choice/lower prices
   - easy to buy
3. Prolems
   - security/technology

Methods of organization

There are many different ways to structure information. Here are some common techniques.

1. The pyramid

Begin with the most general information and move steadily to detail. Reports and promotional literature use this method.

General statement
More specific
Details

Our customers expect the best in terms of service quality.
So — we prioritize reliability, availability, and safety in our systems.

You can invert the pyramid, beginning with the specific first. Useful for handling specific problems where rules must be stated.

Last week a member of staff parked in the CEO's parking space.
May I remind staff that there are spaces reserved for senior management.
Any further incidents of this nature will be dealt with severely.

2. Chronology – report in the time frame of real events

The negotiation went well __yesterday__. We managed to agree to quantities and price. We spent a lot of time __today__ sorting out terms of payment and a timetable for delivery. We should be in a position to sign the contract __tomorrow__.

3. Moving from problem to solution

Several users have reported that their new passwords no longer allow them to access the Intranet. The problem was caused by a software error. Please enter and confirm a new password with a minimum of seven, not six characters.

4. Process sequence

To activate VoiceMail from Sweden:
1. Dial 134
2. Listen to the information message
3. Activate VoiceMail by pressing 1

Make it clear
This instructional format lists points making it clear and easy to read.

5. Classic story-telling – have a beginning, a middle and an end

Many letters use this three-paragraph format which is clear and concise.

I'm sorry that I wasn't able to make the meeting last Friday.

Unfortunately, we had a major problem at our plant in Berlin which I had to solve.

Fortunately, I managed to sort things out. I will be in Paris next week as planned and look forward to seeing you in order to finalize the outsourcing issue.

I   =   Introduction
II =   Development
III =   Conclusion

D I A L O G

Fill in the blanks. Listen and check.

practical	report	sort out	brainstorm

Linda: This incident has really started me thinking.

Mark: You mean the message on the bulletin board?

Linda: Yeah. I want to write a response to it, but I'm still trying to _____ my thoughts. If you're free for lunch, maybe you can help me _____ ideas.

Mark: I could list a few problems with employee accountability for you right now.

Linda: Save them for lunch. Once we get them on paper we can prioritize them and then try to come up with _____ ways to deal with each one.

Mark: If the ideas we come up with are good, Bob may want us to do a formal _____.

V O C A B U L A R Y

Label each example according to the kind of organization it shows.

pyramid	chronology	process

1. _____ employee benefits, medical insurance, insurance company choices

2. _____ history of company to be posted on company website

3. _____ how to install a new software program

4. _____ minutes from a meeting

5. _____ report on employee safety and common accidents at work

P R A C T I C E

Fill in the flow chart for organizing information before you write.

brainstorm	choose method of organization	
decided objective of writing	fill in details	outline report

1. [_____] → 2. [_____]

3. [_____]

4. [_____] → 5. [_____]

3. The business letter – layout

NOUNS
body
closure
context
element
layout
letterhead
reference
regards
salutation
signature

VERBS
enclose
intend

ADJECTIVES
adequate
consistent
dear
justified
optional
standard

ADVERBS
faithfully
sincerely
truly

Many companies have an in-house writing style. The layout below is one example, containing all the elements of a business letter.

INTERNET CONSULTANTS — printed letterhead

136 Madison Avenue, Orlando, Florida 637, USA
Telephone 0304 888587 Fax 0304 8885888
E-mail out.con@aul.com

reference —
Your ref: BD646
Our ref: SF9598   December 12, 2004

US Date
December 12, 2004

Open punctuation is used with no commas or full stops for address, date, references, salutations and closures.

name and
address of
addressee —
Mr Gytes
Managing Director
Technology Conferences
California 89846

salutation — Dear Mr Gytes:

Optional heading makes the subject of the letter clear.

Internet 2005 Conference

Explains reason for writing. / main body of letter —
Following your letter of 10 December, I am writing to confirm that I can speak at next year's conference.

I intend to talk about our new XDSL modems and enclose a preliminary proposal for your attention.

Standard business style: vocabulary and phrases.

Please reserve a room for me at the Darwin Hotel.

The positive and polite close is left justified. —
I look forward to seeing you next year.

It's easy to read with consistent and adequate spacing,

Sincerely yours — closure

signature —

Jeremy Comfortable —
CEO

Encs shows that a document is enclosed. —
encs

Name and professional title. If you see *p.p.* next to a signature, the letter was signed on behalf of another person.

c.c. shows that a copy has been sent to Peter Richards. —
c.c.
Peter Richards, XDSL Product Manager

Context	Salutation	Closure
You don't know the name	Dear Sir Dear Madam Dear Sir / Madam Dear Sirs Gentlemen [US only]	Yours faithfully [UK only] Sincerely yours [US] Yours truly [US] Sincerely [US] Yours sincerely [US]
You know the name	Dear Mr Smith Dear Mr and Mrs Smith Dear Ms Smith* Dear Mrs Smith [married] Dear Miss Smith [single]	Yours sincerely *In British and US English Ms is common for both married and unmarried women*
You know someone quite well	Dear John Dear Angela	Best regards / Regards Best wishes

LETTER

Fill in the blanks. Listen and check.

standard	intended	adequate	Sincerely

June 24, 2003

Dear Sir/Madam:

I bought a Fun Flash 300X Disposable Camera at a local retailer. I _____
to use the Fun Flash 300X at a friend's wedding, but when I developed the
pictures, nothing came out. I was shooting in _____ light in
_____ conditions. The photo store said the problem was in the
camera's manufacturing. I am writing to bring this manufacturing problem to
your attention and to ask for a refund. I am enclosing a copy of my receipt.

I look forward to your prompt response.

_____ ,

Linda Strait

VOCABULARY

Match each word with the correct definition.

1. body
2. layout
3. letterhead
4. salutation
5. signature

a. company name and address at the top of a page
b. greeting
c. how the parts are arranged
d. main information in a letter
e. name written at the bottom of a letter

PRACTICE

Fill in the blanks using the following words.

adequate	consistent	justified	optional	standard

1. Her work is not always _____. Sometimes it is good, and other times it is bad.

2. I prefer letters that are _____ only along the left margin, not both margins.

3. Our company has a _____ format for writing business letters to customers.

4. The letter is informal, so it is _____ to write your job title below your name.

5. This is not the best letter I've seen, but it is _____ for our needs.

4. Correspondence phrases

Vocabulary

NOUNS
assistance
correspondence
expression
inconvenience

VERBS
apologize
contact
enclose
hesitate
inform
look forward to
regret

ADJECTIVES
acceptable
conversational
direct
elaborate
further
grateful
indirect
old-fashioned

ADVERBS
deeply
unfortunately

Starting

With reference to your letter dated 12 January,...
Regarding our meeting last week,...
Thank you for your letter of ... (date)
Re your fax,...

Reason for writing

We are writing to ...
I'm just writing to ...
Just a short note to ...

request
confirm
inform
ask
check

Giving good news

We are delighted to inform you that ....
You will be pleased to hear that ....
You'll be happy to learn that ....

Giving bad news

We regret to inform you that ....
I am afraid that ... / Unfortunately,...
I'm sorry but ....

Making a request

We would appreciate it if you could ...?
I'd be grateful if you could ...?
Could you ...?

Offering help

If you wish, we would be happy to ....
Would you like me to ...? / Shall I ...?
Do you want me to ...?

Apologizing

We must apologize for (not) .... / We deeply regret ....
I do apologize for ... (any inconvenience caused.)
I'm really sorry for / about ....

Enclosing documents

We are enclosing .... / We enclose ....
Please find enclosed ....
I'm enclosing .... / I've enclosed ....

Closing remarks

Do not hesitate to contact us again if you need further assistance.
If you have any further questions, please contact me.
Let me know if you need any more help.

Don't Forget! – Thank you for your help.

Positive future reference

We look forward to meeting / seeing you next week.
We look forward to hearing from you.

Style
There are three major styles of writing:
formal - standard - informal.
Most business correspondence uses a standard style, with elements of the other two styles, depending on the reader.

Which style is the best?

- Write according to your reader!
- Don't be too formal!
- Don't be too informal!
- Be professional!

Legal Contracts

Formal Language
Old-fashioned phrases
Long, elaborate words
Impersonal and indirect tone
Highly structured
Perfect grammar/punctuation

Reports

Standard Professional Language
More direct phrases
Less formal vocabulary
More personal and direct in style
Structured
Perfect grammar/punctuation

Internal E-mail

Informal Language
Conversational expression
Everyday words
Personal style – close to reader
Less structure
Less than perfect grammar and
pronunciation is acceptable

After writing checklist!
- clear objective
- good organization
- professional layout
- clear, concise language
- right style
- correct facts and figures
- all questions answered
- positive ending
- right grammar, spelling
  and punctuation!

Short forms
- be consistent
- don't use for formal
  writing

L E T T E R

Fill in the blanks. Listen and check.

grateful	contact	enclosing	apologize

Fun Flash Cameras
7750 Beltway St., Carson, OH 44277, USA
phone: (365)972-3350 fax: (365)972-3351

June 30, 2003

Dear Ms. Strait:

We regret the problem you experienced with the Fun Flash 300X. We are
_____ for your bringing this problem to our attention. The manufacturing
problem has been corrected. We _____ for the inconvenience this has
caused you.

We are _____ a refund and another two Fun Flash 300X Disposable
Cameras. We hope that you will use them and see the true quality of our products.
Please do not hesitate to _____ us if you have any more problems.

Sincerely,

Kevin Stills
Customer Service

V O C A B U L A R Y

Connect the parts to make complete sentences.

1. Feel free to contact me ...
2. I am very grateful ...
3. Please find enclosed ...
4. We apologize for ...
5. We regret to inform you ...

a. a full refund for your purchase.
b. if you have further questions.
c. for all the help you have given me.
d. your application was rejected.
e. any inconvenience this has caused.

P R A C T I C E

Mark the type of document described by each style.

STYLE	LEGAL CONTRACT	REPORT	E-MAIL
1. conversational tone	( )	( )	( )
2. old-fashioned, elaborate words	( )	( )	( )
3. standard vocabulary, direct style	( )	( )	( )
4. impersonal and indirect	( )	( )	( )
5. grammar like spoken language	( )	( )	( )

5. Model letters

Explaining a delay   Confirming a contract   Placing an order   Complaining   Requesting payment
Asking for overdue payment   Accepting an invitation   Booking a hotel room   Asking for a price

NOUNS
confirmation
explanation
payment
scenario
solution
strategy

VERBS
adapt
book
confirm
enclose
hesitate
hold a meeting
pick up
reassess

ADJECTIVES
convenient
immediate
latest
model
overdue

One strategy to improve your writing is to prepare model letters which you can use many times for key scenarios. Some examples are given below.
Simply adapt them to your needs!

Organizing a meeting

I am writing to organize our next MCP meeting to reassess our current marketing strategy for the E258. — Clear statement of the reason for writing

I am free to travel to Germany between June 13 and 15. — Date proposed

Please let me know as soon as possible if these dates are convenient. — Confirmation request

Agreeing to a meeting

Thank you for the reminder about the MCP meeting! — Friendly, informal reference

I think it would be best if you flew in on Monday, June 13 and we hold the meeting on Tuesday. If we begin at 9:00, I'm sure we'll be finished by 3:30. — Clear proposal

Please confirm your arrival details so that I can arrange for someone to pick you up at the airport. I will book a room for you at the Sheraton, as usual. — Polite request and offer of help

Confirming travel details

Regarding our MCP meeting in June, I am writing with my travel details. — Clear reference and reason for writing

I arrive in Frankfurt at 09:30 on Monday, June 13. I will take a taxi and plan to be at your office by 10:15. — Concise information

If there are any problems, you can reach me on 00441904-769009. — Contact details

I look forward to seeing you. — Positive close

Requesting information

I am writing to request a copy of the instructors' manual for the E10 and S12. — Clear request

Please could you also send me a copy of your new brochure and price list? — Good style. Uses *could you* to avoid repeating request

Sending information

With reference to your enquiry of July 15, I am enclosing two copies each of the E10 and S12 instructors' manuals. You will also find enclosed our latest brochure and price list. — Clear reference

Please do not hesitate to contact us if you need further information. — Polite, formal offer of help

Raising a problem

To: IS Department
I am having problems accessing the Intranet from my desktop. — Definition of the problem
When I enter my password, the screen freezes and will not re-boot.

Could you please solve this problem as soon as possible? — Polite request for immediate help

Problem solving

To: Joe User
The Intranet access problem was caused by a password corruption error. — Clear explanation of the problem
Please enter CLEAR as a password next time you access the Intranet. — Clear solution to the problem
Then, key in your new password – SMART.

If you have any further problems, please contact me immediately. — Polite, informal offer of help

L E T T E R

Fill in the blanks. Listen and check.

convenient	confirm	payment	hold

Dear Ms. Strait,

This letter is to _____ your registration at the annual training workshop to be held in Chicago. We have enclosed a separate page listing hotels near the training center where we will _____ the workshop. Please book your room early.

This confirmation letter is a notice that we have listed you as attending. However, full _____ for the workshop must be received before Aug. 1. Payments made after this date will result in overdue fees being added to the registration fee. Please feel free to use our _____ on-line payment service provided through the workshop website.

We look forward to seeing you in Chicago!

Sincerely,

Janet Davis
Training Coordinator

V O C A B U L A R Y

Match the phrases with similar meanings.

1. make a payment
2. find a solution
3. give confirmation
4. make a reservation
5. outline a strategy

a. book a room
b. fix it
c. give a plan
d. say it arrived
e. send money

P R A C T I C E

What kind of reply should you write? Write the type of letter in the blank.

accepting	complaining	explaining	confirming	requesting

1. A client has asked to set up a meeting. _____

2. You want information on the latest software from a company. _____

3. A customer was over charged due to a computer problem. _____

4. Your company did not receive the correct order. _____

5. A speaker has agreed to give a workshop at your company. _____

6. Writing clearly – extra points

Vocabulary

NOUNS
abbreviation
acronym
caption
cliché
competitor
context
figure
font
header
illustration
jargon
margin
option
survival guide
tone
topic sentence
white space

VERBS
bullet
commence
package
present
reprimand
terminate

ADJECTIVES
abbreviated
bold
consistent
dynamic
justified
plain
relevant
specific
sufficient
underlined

ADVERBS
absolutely
strongly

You must always present your message clearly and adapt your style and tone according to your objective, the specific reader and the business context.

Language

- Keep sentences short and focused.
- Use plain and simple vocabulary.
- Begin and/or end paragraphs with key ideas············> = topic sentences!
- Avoid jargon, abbreviations, acronyms and cliché.
- Make sure headers are clear and concise.
- Vary the beginnings of sentences and paragraphs.
- Don't repeat!

✗ _Please could you_ send me report 667/Ab?
Please could you also let me know the meeting agenda for Friday?

Formatting – keep readers smiling

- Ensure that spacing is consistent and sufficient.
- Maintain wide margins, nothing less than 2.5 cm.
- Avoid long paragraphs. Use headers and sub-headers in bold or underlined.
- Write lists as bullet points.
- Use a maximum of 2 or 3 fonts in long documents.
- Develop a clear and consistent numbering system.

Graphics

- Use a graph, diagram, chart or illustration, to clarify and highlight key information.
- Number and caption each graphic.
- Refer to illustrations as **Figures** (abbreviated to Fig.)
- Keep graphics close to the relevant part of the text.
- Set graphics in plenty of white space.

Tone

- Ask yourself:
  – why am I writing?·················
  – what do I want to achieve?
- Be polite and professional at all times.
- Package negative content by starting and ending with something positive.

Examples of plain English

~~advise~~ tell	~~prior to~~ before
~~commence~~ start	~~per annum~~ a year
~~complete~~ fill in	~~terminate~~ end

In the future, we will have to change. Traditional business relationships are being redefined by e-commerce. In addition, dynamic new competitors have entered the market. _The following represents a survival guide...._

The perfect format

Fully justified
Wide margin
Professional font

Most companies use their own stationery for faxes, similar to a memo in layout.

Faxes can sometimes be less formal than business letters.

Oct Nov Dec
Fig. 6 Sales 2003

Reasons for writing	Tone
To reprimand	Strict
To give information	Neutral
To get feedback	Open

Communicate your opinion by selecting the right phrase!

	Recommending
Strong	We strongly recommend that .... We are absolutely convinced that ....
Neutral	We recommend that .... We expect that ....
Weak	One option may be to .... We could consider ....

LETTER

Fill in the blanks. Listen and check.

captions	jargon	absolutely	consistent

To: Tim Grayson
From: Linda Strait
RE: Employee Accountability Report recommendations

Dear Tim,

Thanks for looking at our report on Employee Accountability and offering suggestions to improve it. Mark and I agree that using plain language and less _____ will make the report clearer. We were also not aware that the fonts were not _____ throughout the report. Thanks for pointing that out! Mark is going to work on the _____ for the figures, so he'll probably check with you later in the week to make sure they are all _____ clear to readers.

Thanks again for your suggestions.

Sincerely,

Linda Strait
Sales Representative

VOCABULARY

Circle the word that does not belong in each group.

1. cliché   line spacing   margin   page number
2. present   reprimand   show   tell
3. bold   italic   justified   underlined
4. detailed   dynamic   exact   specific
5. figure   graphic   illustration   option

PRACTICE

Circle the best word to complete the sentence.

1. I _____ recommend that you check the report one more time before you submit it.
   a. deeply   b. sincerely   c. strongly   d. unfortunately

2. The _____ includes the title of the document, the writer's name, and the page number.
   a. context   b. header   c. margin   d. tone

3. The first name is _____ in the letter, so I don't know if the writer is a man or a woman.
   a. abbreviated   b. consistent   c. relevant   d. sufficient

4. This list would be easier to read if you _____ each item.
   a. bulleted   b. commenced   c. packaged   d. terminated

5. What does the _____ NASA stand for?
   a. acronym   b. caption   c. topic   d. sentence

7. The business report – layout

NOUNS
appendix / appendices
background
deadline
executive summary
feedback
indentation
investigation
layout
limitation
recommendation
scope
structure
table
title
type size

VERBS
debrief
integrate
justify
launch

ADJECTIVES
alphabetical
ample
fixed
fundamental
relative

ADVERBS
clearly
logically
thoroughly

debriefing   memo   research   budget   project   conference   approval

There are many different layouts for business reports. Again, you must write according to your company's in-house style.

Debriefing reports

– to report on a conference, a meeting or a visit
You could organize a debriefing report using the following headers:

Where/When	Why	Who	What
Geneva Telecoms August 10-11, 2003	Product launch	New contacts: name, function	Action points

Informal reports

– to update people on projects, budgets, etc.
There is no fixed format. Simply present information clearly and logically.

Research reports

– to present findings of research / investigation

Title page
Include title, name of writer, date and reference.

Contents list
Include all headings / sub-headings with page numbers. Indentation and type size is used to show relative importance of headers.

(Executive) summary
Review key points. People will then decide if they should read the report.

Methods of investigation
Explain how you researched the report and, therefore, how you justify your conclusions.

Introduction
State the report's objective, scope and limitations.

The body of the report
Present findings, recommendations and conclusions, often with separate headings / sub-headings.

Appendices
Include tables of figures, illustrations, etc.

References
Number references to sources. Then list them at the end of sections.

Index
List key words in alphabetical order with page number of use.

Report checklist – ask yourself!
Before writing
What is the objective?
What will interest the reader?
What background should I give?
How should I structure the information?
When is the deadline?
Which layout is best?
How do I organize my data?

After writing
Is it concise and relevant?
Have I checked it thoroughly?
What are my key recommendations?
Who can I ask for feedback?

Report extract –
6.0 Recommendations
E-commerce promises to have a fundamental impact, although it is difficult as yet to predict when, where and to what degree change will occur. However, there are clear strategies which suppliers must adopt in order to meet this challenge.

6.1 Technology
Suppliers must embrace and prioritize new technology by adopting new training strategies.

6.2 Customers
Suppliers must move closer to key customers and further integrate their businesses.

Reader-friendly writing
■ Consistent and ample spacing
■ Clear headings and sub-headings
■ Single font with bold for focus
■ Short and focused sections
■ Justified and indented text
■ Clear numbering system

R E P O R T

Fill in the blanks. Listen and check.

appendices	feedback	investigation	recommendations

Executive Summary

In response to a recent message posted within the department, an _____ of employee attitudes toward accountability in the company was launched. The investigation was done through a survey in which employees could give _____ to a list of questions with fixed responses on a scale. Employees were also asked to provide _____ for improving accountability. Employee responses are listed in the tables in the _____. This report discusses the findings of the survey along with the obvious limitations of this study.

V O C A B U L A R Y

Find a noun in the Vocabulary list to complete the definition and write it in the blank.

1. A space at the beginning of a paragraph is called an _____.
2. The date you must finish a project by is called the _____.
3. The information you give first to help people understand a topic is the _____.
4. The label you use to refer to a document or report is the _____.
5. The range of information covered in a report is called the _____ of the report.

P R A C T I C E

Put the following questions and answers in logical order (a=first, e=last).

_____ 1. You're right about that. Do you have any other recommendations?

_____ 2. You should also use a larger type size and justify along both margins.

_____ 3. Thanks a lot. All of your ideas are really helpful.

_____ 4. Which layout do you prefer?

_____ 5. I like the one with more white space to give ample room for people to write notes.

8. Connecting words

Vocabulary

NOUNS
consequence
contrast
efficiency
flag
recycling
replacement

VERBS
bring about
enable
flag
highlight
recycle

ADJECTIVES
above-mentioned
effective
former
latter
partial

ADVERBS
consequently
respectively
similarly

The secret of effective writing is to connect words, sentences and paragraphs together to enable the reader to understand quickly and easily.

Connectors

Connectors link words and phrases, for example, *however* and *as a result of*. They are signals to the reader of the relationship between ideas. For example, *as a result* introduces the cause of something

• sequencing	first, second, third, after that, finally
• adding	in addition, moreover, furthermore
• alternatives	alternatively, instead of
• consequence	therefore, consequently, as a result
• comparing	similarly, in line with
• contrasting	however, yet, whereas, although, despite
• conditions	if, on condition that, providing, unless
• reference	with respect to, regarding, in relation to
• reasons	because, since, as, in response to
• cause verbs	to lead to, to result in, to bring about, to cause
• effect verbs	to result from, to be due to, to be caused by
• highlighting	in particular, especially, mainly, chiefly
• exemplifying	for example/ instance, such as, as follows
• generalizing	usually, normally, in general

> **As a result of** improved sales, we are able to offer staff a very healthy profit share

> We finished on time
> ⸹
> **despite** several delays
> ⸹
> **due to** bad weather

Replacement words

Replacement words, for example, *who, this, the former*, are used to refer to people, ideas and things already mentioned in a text. Although **partial recycling** of key words may link a text effectively, style and efficiency are improved by avoiding too much repetition.

Sales were well above target. This means we can offer a very healthy profit share.

Replacement words	it/they/them one/ones respectively	this/that these/those such	the former/the latter who/which/that

Text flags

To improve the clarity of texts, we sometimes need to refer back or forward.

The **above-mentioned** quality system will come into effect in July.

> **Text flags**
> above/below   in paragraph 10.1
> as mentioned earlier   the above-mentioned ....
> the previous/following   as follows   on page 12

REPORT

Fill in the blanks. Listen and check.

efficiency	effective	bring about	above-mentioned

Recommendations

Many employees felt the most _____ way to improve individual accountability was through special recognition in each department. Employees with exceptional _____ or outstanding performance can be recognized through "Employee of the Month" awards. Highlighting the performance of employees with good personal accountability may _____ improved performance throughout each department. Consequently, efficiency and performance throughout the whole company will increase.

The _____ recommendation is the most common idea. A partial list of the other ideas listed by employees in the survey can be found in Appendix D.

VOCABULARY

Fill in the blanks using the correct connector.

For example	However	In addition	In particular	Therefore

1. Companies are using the Internet to provide information to customers. _____, many companies are now marketing products on-line.
2. I need to see our customer file for Mega Mall. _____, I need their account statements for last year.
3. Let's decorate the office for the party. _____, we can hang a banner over the door.
4. The distribution problem has been solved. _____, another problem has come up.
5. We have received many complaints about the product. _____, the product should be taken off the market.

PRACTICE

Choose the correct words for the following text.

From a report "Forecast — English Language Teaching"

Several key developments will emerge in the near future. (First, Next), teachers will have to become more qualified. (This, These) will be in response both to a demand from employers seeking higher professionalism, (and, or) to competition from increasing numbers of students trying to enter programs.

(After that, Second), the status of teachers who are non-native English speakers will rise, (especially, similarly) in eastern European countries unable to afford western professionals. The following graph shows . . .

9. E-mail

Vocabulary

NOUNS
address book
attachment
capitals
caution
colleague
ellipsis
file
filing system
medium
signature
subject box
subordinate
variation

VERBS
abuse
delete
forward
frown
over-use
print
reply
retain
retrieve
think twice
tilt
wink

ADJECTIVES
confidential
offensive
personal
precise
previous
private
up-to-date

ADVERBS
ASAP
daily
informally
legally
primarily

The Good E-mailer

- keeps messages short
- presents information clearly with bullet points
- enters a precise subject in the subject box
- doesn't over-use the "reply" function
- checks their mail box at least three times daily
- limits personal mail and small talk
- gives people time to reply
- doesn't forward mail without thinking
- creates a filing system for mail/attachments
- reports offensive mail
- adds key information in the e-mail signature
- never abuses the system for private messages
- thinks twice about attaching very large files
- telephones if an immediate answer is required
- keeps address book up-to-date
- is professional at all times

I'm Bad

I write too informally.
I write in capitals for effect.
I send huge attachments.
I love abbreviations/symbols.
I use e-mail to avoid phoning.
I send offensive material.
I print every e-mail.

How do I write e-mails?

E-mail is primarily <u>a medium</u> rather than <u>a style</u> of communication. People write e-mails in many different styles, depending on corporate policy and on whether they are writing a business letter to a client, a memo to subordinates or a note to colleagues. Some features of informal e-mail communication are shown below to save you time when writing informally to colleagues.

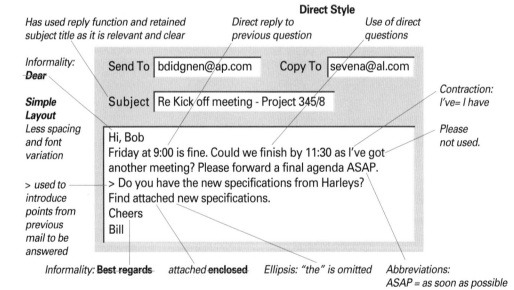

Direct Style

Has used reply function and retained subject title as it is relevant and clear

Direct reply to previous question

Use of direct questions

Informality: ~~Dear~~

Simple Layout Less spacing and font variation

> used to introduce points from previous mail to be answered

Send To | bdidgnen@ap.com   Copy To | sevena@al.com

Subject | Re Kick off meeting - Project 345/8

Hi, Bob
Friday at 9:00 is fine. Could we finish by 11:30 as I've got another meeting? Please forward a final agenda ASAP.
> Do you have the new specifications from Harleys?
Find attached new specifications.
Cheers
Bill

Contraction: I've= I have

Please not used.

Informality: ~~Best regards~~   attached ~~enclosed~~   Ellipsis: "the" is omitted   Abbreviations: ASAP = as soon as possible

Big brother/sister is watching you

E-mail is not a private way of communicating. Employers have the right to access your mail. Deleted mail can be retrieved by experts. Use caution when communicating confidential or legally sensitive information. Make sure you know who will read the information you are sending.

Smileys are symbols used to communicate your mood by indicating facial expressions. Tilt your head to the left and you see the face:
:-) = smile   ;-) = wink   :-(= frown
:-D = laugh   :-X = no comment

E - M A I L

Fill in the blanks. Listen and check.

print	personal	retrieving	attachment

To: lstrait@biz.com
From: tgray@biz.com
CC: markmark@biz.com
Subject: Re: Employee Accountability report

Hi Linda,
I was glad to hear the report was well accepted. Please send me the document file as
an _____. I'd like to _____ the final version of the report and keep
a copy of it in my _____ files. I've had some problems _____
attachments through my mail box at work. Reply to my other account at
oldtimer@ola.com.
Thanks,
Tim

V O C A B U L A R Y

Match each smileys (or emoticons) with the correct meaning.

1. :)   a. frowning face - I'm sad.

2. :(b. smiling face - I'm happy.

3. ;)   c. tongue out - I'm teasing.

4. :o   d. winking face - Get it?

5. :P   e. surprised face - Oh no! Oh my!

P R A C T I C E

Circle the word with a similar meaning as the underlined words.

1. A fax will be better than e-mail because the company needs your <u>signed name</u>.
   a. address   b. ellipsis   c. medium   d. signature

2. Please <u>erase</u> this message after you read it.
   a. delete   b. forward   c. retain   d. tilt

3. She asked him to reply to her message <u>at the earliest possible time</u>.
   a. ASAP   b. P.S.   c. CC   d. Re

4. When you write using all <u>large letters</u>, people read it as shouting.
   a. capitals   b. caution   c. colleague   d. communication

5. You can download a <u>recent</u> version of the program for free.
   a. confidential   b. previous   c. precise   d. up-to-date

10. The perfect résumé

Vocabulary

NOUNS
ability
accomplishment
capability
competence
competency
distinction
duplicate
guidelines
margin
résumé
spacing
typography

VERBS
attract
demonstrate
double space
employ
exceed
indent
overuse
quote
tailor

ADJECTIVES
centered
chronological
internal
irrelevant
justified
recent
well-structured

ADVERBS
grammatically

Follow the guidelines below and write a résumé to attract employers and make them want to employ you.

A good résumé is ...

- Well-structured
- Short, simple and clear
- Easy to read and professional-looking
- Tailored to the job and the employer
- Focused on results not simply competency
- Free of irrelevant detail
- Without spelling and punctuation errors
- Grammatically perfect

> Don't include hobbies and interests unless they demonstrate relevant job qualities.

> One page is best. Two is maximum.

> Quote figures and statistics to enhance your achievements.

TRISHA SPOTT
635 Fort Apache Road North Bay,
NY 25626 (206) 575-8775

TARGET JOB Telecoms engineer - Research and Development

CAPABILITIES Design and testing of terminal equipment
Application of R&D findings to new equipment
Project management 3676/affg

ACCOMPLISHMENTS
Designed and tested GSM/UMTS interface
Implemented security 465/AA system
Redrafted ITU panel ITU/768

WORK HISTORY
1995 - Present   TELENORIA: 136 80 Haninge, Sweden
Assistant Head of R&D
1993-1995   ALCABEL: 67476 Vélizy, France
Chief Engineer, R&D

EDUCATION
1989-1993   ENST: Paris, France
Advanced Radio Engineering Diploma
1986   London Institute of Telecommunications
B.Sc. - Electrical Engineering (with distinction)

The covering letter – some ideas

- Write to the responsible person, not Dear Sir/Madam
- Demonstrate knowledge of the company
- Communicate your competence and sell your value
- Ask for an interview

Perfect Formatting

Typography
For titles and headings, use
UPPERCASE

Don't overuse
Italics **Bold** <u>Underline</u>

Personal details
Name, address etc. must be
centered or left justified
at the top.

Space
Wide margins
Double spacing
Indents

**The tailored résumé –
clear and focused**
This type of résumé focuses on
where your abilities match or exceed
the target job, and it lists only those
capabilities/accomplishments
relevant to the position.

Make sure you use a
laser printer or a quality
copy shop for duplicates.

Other Résumés

1. Chronological
<u>Headings</u>
- work history
- education
- supporting data

2. Competence
<u>Headings</u>
- skills/results
- work history
- education

3. Internal
<u>Headings</u>
- introduction
- capabilities
- achievements
- recent training
- recent work history

D I A L O G

Fill in the blanks. Listen and check.

attract	tailor	well-structured	accomplishments

Mark: Did you have a chance to look over my résumé, Linda?

Linda: Yes, I did, Mark. I thought it was very _____ and follows all the guidelines for a good résumé I learned in college.

Mark: I tried to _____ it to the management job I'm applying for.

Linda: You did a great job. All of the experience you listed really demonstrates your _____ in this department. And I think it shows your capability as an organizer and manager.

Mark: What about the fonts and spacing? And how about the color of this paper? Does it _____ your attention?

V O C A B U L A R Y

Match each word with the correct definition.

1. employ
2. exceed
3. overuse
4. quote
5. tailor

a. go beyond or above
b. use another person's words
c. hire someone to work for you
d. make to fit a special need or purpose
e. use too much

P R A C T I C E

Put the following headings in the correct place on the résumé.

Education	Objective	Work Experience	References	Skills

Sue Brown

101 Main St., Weston, MN 98244

(703)775-8100

1) _____ : Obtain an entrance level sales and marketing position

2) _____ : Bachelor's in Economics, State University, MN   May 2002

3) _____ : Student Manager

University Book Store   Aug 2001 - May 2002

assigned work schedule, inventory and stocking, sales

4) _____ : creating spreadsheets, word processing, accounting machines

5) _____ : available upon request

11. Grammar and spelling check

Vocabulary

NOUNS
advice
comma
mistake
reputation
tense

VERBS
damage
edit
identify
misspell
rely on

ADJECTIVES
countable
general
individual
non-essential
poor

ADVERBS
correctly
wrongly

Poor grammar and spelling are unprofessional and can damage the reputation of both the writer and his or her company. Edit your own writing with the following checklist!

Checklist	Common mistakes
Tense	The goods ~~have~~ arrived yesterday.
Verb number	My people ~~is~~ are highly trained.
Countable or not	Please e-mail ~~these datas~~ this data.
Modal verbs	We must ~~to~~ solve this problem soon.
If	If I ~~would have~~ had money, I would travel more.
Adverb or adjective	Please follow the ~~normally~~ normal procedure.
Position of the adverb	We always have ~~always~~ this problem.
Preposition	We must focus ~~at~~ on this at the next meeting.
Key words e.g. *since*	He ~~is working~~ has been working here **since** July.
False friends	The ~~actual~~ current inflation rate is 3%.

WHO for people/WHICH for things

1. We need a technician who is familiar with Unix.
2. Peter James, who is currently in Japan, will lead the project team.

which / that = things

1. We have identified the circuit board that is faulty.
2. The new strategy, which was agreed on by the whole board, has proved to be a great success.

> Commas are used when you add non-essential information.

Spelling – don't believe your eyes

Don't rely on the computer spell check. It will **not** tell you if you have misspelled a name, place or product. It will also **fail** to identify words which are spelled correctly but wrongly used. Can you correct the underlined errors in the text below?

I was delighted to <u>here</u> that you took my <u>advise</u> and bought a new English dictionary. <u>Their</u> very useful and will help you <u>too</u> practice your spelling. I think you know that spelling is your <u>principle</u> weakness. The dictionary will help you identify <u>you're</u> mistakes and <u>were</u> you must improve!

American		British	
Important general differences			
labor	-or	labour	-our
catalog	-og	catalogue	-ogue
center	-er	centre	-tre
program	-gram	programme	-gramme
canceled	-led	cancelled	-lled
Important individual differences			
check		cheque	
defense		defence	
practice (verb or noun)		practise (verb)	
		practice (noun)	
through / thru		through	

Don't rely too much on spell check

> Don't worry. The spell check will correct any mistakes.

GOLDEN ADVICE
Ask a colleague to check your writing.

Fill in the blanks. Listen and check.

reputation	advice	rely on	non-essential

Mark: Can you check the spelling and punctuation for me one more time? I had a _____ as a terrible speller in school, so I always worry about it now.

Linda: I usually _____ my computer to check all that for me.

Mark: That works well in general, but I've noticed a few times the computer has suggested I've wrongly written a sentence that is actually correct.

Linda: I've noticed that too. Usually the problem is related to the use of _____ commas.

Mark: I trust your _____ more than a computer. Do you see anything to edit in my résumé?

V O C A B U L A R Y

Mark each statement as using either American or British spelling.

	AMERICAN	**BRITISH**
1. He practiced his speech several times before the meeting.	( )	( )
2. She requested a catalogue from the company's website.	( )	( )
3. The bank refused to make payment on the cheque.	( )	( )
4. The labor union went on strike.	( )	( )
5. The workshop will be held in the Darwin Centre.	( )	( )

P R A C T I C E

Correct the mistake in each of the following sentences.

1. I entered all the data correct, but there still seems to be an error.

2. She is researching customer satisfaction for the last two months.

3. The people involved in the negotiation is all from Australia.

4. Your fax has arrived over the weekend when the office was closed.

5. The report must to be finished before next Tuesday.

12. Punctuation

Vocabulary

NOUNS
apostrophe
bracket
break
clause
colon
comma
contraction
correspondence
dash
hyphen
judgment
parenthesis
possession
punctuation
semi-colon
slash

VERBS
contract
punctuate

ADJECTIVES
introductory
separate
subjective
subordinate

Clear and professional writing needs good punctuation. In general, we punctuate less now than in the past, with more room for personal style, especially in informal communication.

The comma

1. <u>After introductory word(s)</u>
   Technically speaking, it is possible to repair the machine.
   As requested, I am attaching the COM file.

2. <u>To separate items in a list</u>
   Our people will identify, analyze and solve the problem.

3. <u>To create breaks in a sentence</u>
   a. As a parenthesis (the sentence can stand without the part between the commas)
      The project, despite some setbacks, ran exactly to schedule.
      The big problem, which all agreed, was how to cut costs.
   b. As a natural break for the reader
      The existing software has crashed several times, leading to severe operational difficulties.

> **!** Rules for <u>natural breaks</u> are not easy to give as 'natural' is a subjective judgment. It is more important to remember to keep sentences short. Don't overuse commas to create very long sentences.

No comma for the address, date, salutation and closing phrase!

No commas before subordinate clauses! *She said that ̖ it was ...* ✗

No comma after please at the beginning of a sentence! *Please ̖ confirm in writing.* ✗

The colon – introduces a list of items

We must clarify three key issues: manpower, deadlines and finance.
But in terms of style and clarity, a bullet point list is sometimes better.

The semi-colon – connects two sentences which are closely related.

BUILDCOM wants a meeting; they are worried about the delay.

The apostrophe

1. **For possession/relationship**

Human	President Bush's decision
Organization	The company's strength
Location	Japan's trading partner

2. **To contract two words**
   Contraction is used for less formal business correspondence.

Apostrophe with time
A week's time
In two months' time
Three years' time

I've	she's	we're
we'd	won't	we'll
shouldn't		can't

The dash – is similar to the comma

1. **As an informal parenthesis**
   The meeting was postponed – to everyone's annoyance – until June.

2. **As an informal natural break**
   Subscribe to UK Telecon today – and buy the best service.

What do you call it?
@ = at
_ = underscore
\ = back slash
[...] = square brackets
/ = slash
— = dash

CAPITAL LETTERS

Beginning of a sentence	Months	Names
Streets	Countries	Days
Nationalities	Languages	

Hyphens
Use hyphens to join words together.
Numbers: thirty-six
Adjectives: up-to-date

D I A L O G

Fill in the blanks. Listen and check.

colon	break	commas	punctuation

Mark: Linda, can you take a look at this and tell me if the _____ is correct?

Linda: Sure, Mark. What do you want me to look at?

Mark: I'm not sure if this sentence needs _____ or not.

Linda: I'm not an expert on this, but I usually use a comma if I would naturally _____ or pause when reading the sentence out loud. In this case, you have an introductory phrase in the sentence. Put a comma here after the phrase.

Mark: And what about this other sentence. Should I use a _____ or semi-colon?

Linda: Use a colon before a list and a semi-colon between sentences. You need a semi-colon here.

V O C A B U L A R Y

Add commas to the following sentences. Some sentences need more than one comma.

1. As part of the sales team you will need to know how to use our filing system.

2. Because we missed the deadline we did not get the contract.

3. Everyone thought the advertisements were beautiful but they were still not effective.

4. Refreshments at the meeting included coffee tea muffins and fruit.

5. Bob who manages the sales department has been with the company for twelve years.

P R A C T I C E

Answers these questions with complete sentences. Use capital letters where necessary.

1. What is your full name?

   _____

2. What is your nationality?

   _____

3. When were you born? (Give month, day, and year.)

   _____

4. Which languages can you speak?

   _____

5. Which city and country would you like to live in outside your own country?

   _____

13. Getting technical

Vocabulary

NOUNS
ability
content
depth
facility
height
length
structure
task
volume
weight
width

VERBS
accommodate
activate
adjust
alter
be composed of
comprise
consist of
contain
enable
initiate
modify
operate
perform
permit
press
recalibrate
take care of
terminate

ADJECTIVES
critical
immobilized
impersonal
protective
rare
technical

ADVERBS
simultaneously

Describing systems

Below are some key verbs – and their synonyms – which will help you with your technical writing. Use them to develop a database of key words.

Concept	Verbs and synonyms	
Structure	Our system <u>is made up of</u> four different parts.	comprise, consist of, be composed of
Facility	The ADAN system <u>lets</u> you offer per second billing.	enable, allow, provide, permit
Ability	DETON will <u>deal with</u> problems quickly.	handle, manage, take care of
Tasking	Please <u>carry out</u> this test regularly.	do, perform
Contents	This site can <u>house</u> three electrical units.	contain, accommodate
Change	XDS parameters must be <u>changed</u> by an operator.	adjust, alter, recalibrate

Many functional descriptions use the simple format below:

CD-ROM
1. Disk tray   <u>Opens</u> and <u>closes</u> for disk loading / unloading
2. Volume   <u>Controls</u> volume output for headphones or speakers

Instructions – assembly, installation and operating
The instruction types below are a critical part of technical writing.

1. Procedures

Imperative   **Remove** the housing and **install** the CD-Rom drive.
Must/Should   Surfaces **should** be clean and dry.
To/In order to **To/In order to** operate, press start.

2. Sequence
Most technical writing uses **<u>numbered points</u>** to indicate sequence. You can also use words:
Before/After press<u>ing</u> * key, wait two seconds.
When programming, please wear protective clothing.
The alarm will activate. **Hereafter**, the system is immobilized.
To initiate, begin, start (up),... / To finish, end, terminate,...

3. Conditions – *If* and other expressions
If the alarm activates, contact an engineer immediately.
Set-up may not always be successful. **In this case**, re-start the process.
In rare cases, you may need to contact the technical helpline.

It's Easy!
1. Press * key
2. Enter time

Describing processes with impersonal (passive) grammar

The Sea Mermaid tool is <u>positioned</u> over a bolt and <u>is linked</u> to hydraulic hoses. These <u>are connected</u> to the diving support vessel. Once activated, all the <u>bolts are simultaneously tensioned</u>. When the pressure <u>is released</u>, the tools <u>can be removed</u>.

Complex specifications

TIP! When writing technical specifications, <u>modify</u> the content, format and style of existing corporate documentation in line with your needs.

Dimensions

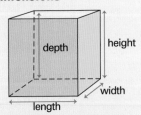

The height is .... / It is ... high.
The length is .... / It is ... long.
The width is .... / It is ... long.
The depth is .... / It is ... deep.
The weight is .... / It weighs ....
The volume is ....

ⓜⓐⓝⓤⓐⓛ

Fill in the blanks. Listen and check.

initiate	critical	press	technical

Installing SalesTrack 5000

Before installing the software, it is _____ to make sure your computer contains adequate memory space and has several applications enabled. Check the _____ specifications listed on the next page to be sure SalesTrack 5000 will run on your computer.

To _____ the installation wizard, load the CD-ROM in your disk drive. If the wizard does not activate automatically, open the window for the CD drive and double-click the EXE file displayed. When the wizard opens, _____ the 'Begin Installation' button by clicking the button on the screen.

ⓥⓞⓒⓐⓑⓤⓛⓐⓡⓨ

Circle the word that does not belong in each group.

1. content   height   length   width

2. adjust   alter   modify   permit

3. ability   competence   skill   volume

4. be composed of   be comprised of   consist of   complain of

5. hit   immobilize   press   push

ⓟⓡⓐⓒⓣⓘⓒⓔ

Choose the best word to complete the sentence.

1. Both parties _____ suggested a solution to the problem.

   a. consequently   b. daily   c. primarily   d. simultaneously

2. It is sometimes necessary to _____ the machine to make it work properly.

   a. comprise   b. contain   c. perform   d. recalibrate

3. Pull here to remove the _____ wrap covering the product.

   a. critical   b. impersonal   c. protective   d. rare

4. The conference room can _____ up to twelve people.

   a. accommodate   b. enable   c. operate   d. terminate

5. It required three workers two days to complete the _____ .

   a. depth   b. structure   c. task   d. weight

14. Golden rules

NOUNS
bias
capital letter
cliché
feedback
font
jargon
model
phrase
prejudice
recommendation
slang
thesaurus

VERBS
edit
emphasize
format
keep in mind
link
minimize
over-use
re-draft
stick to the point

ADVERBS
at all times
badly
logically
thoroughly

Apply the principles and language of this book.

Do

- keep the reader in mind at all stages of writing
- plan thoroughly before you put pen to paper
- let your reader know quickly why you are writing
- organize your ideas clearly and logically
- link ideas, sentences, and paragraphs with connecting language
- format documents in a reader-friendly way in corporate style
- use 100% correct grammar, spelling and punctuation
- minimize your use of jargon, slang and cliché
- support recommendations and ideas with facts
- create interest by using a variety of sentence forms
- always emphasize the positive over the negative
- vary sentence length but keep the average at 18 words
- avoid humor except in very informal correspondence
- remain polite and professional at all times
- be concise and stick to the point
- check any facts and references that you quote
- use a thesaurus to avoid repeating words
- break up long, boring text with headers/sub-headers
- be simple and direct, as if talking to a friend
- ask a friend to check your writing and give you feedback
- make it perfect by editing and re-drafting
- create a personal file of model letters and phrases

Good planning, organization, language and formatting will produce effective business writing.

Don't

- write too much
- think that grammar and punctuation are unimportant
- rely on the computer spell check
- be rude or negative
- repeat too many words and phrases
- try to be humorous
- use sexist language
- over-use capital letters
- forget that badly formatted documents look unprofessional
- use more than two or three fonts in longer documents
- show bias or prejudice
- send an important document without getting feedback first

Have courage! Getting feedback is essential to improve your writing.

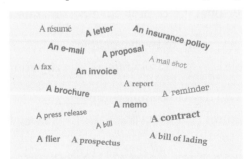

A résumé   A letter   An insurance policy
An e-mail   A proposal
A fax   A mail shot
An invoice
A brochure   A report   A reminder
A memo
A press release   A contract
A bill
A flier   A prospectus   A bill of lading

Learning tip

Read letters you receive carefully and note down useful expressions which you can use.

D I A L O G

Fill in the blanks. Listen and check.

logically	keep in mind	emphasizes	re-drafted

Mark: This is the last time I'll ask you to edit my work, Linda. I promise.

Linda: I don't mind, Mark. How many times have you _____ this document?

Mark: I think this is the third time. But it's getting better, right?

Linda: Oh yeah! The first draft wasn't written badly, but I think the document now communicates your ideas more _____. And the way the ideas are linked is more effective and really _____ what you're trying to say.

Mark: I tried to _____ your recommendations from last time and stick to the point of the document's objective.

V O C A B U L A R Y

Mark each idea as a good idea (DO) or bad idea (DON'T) for a presentation.

	DO	DON'T
1. Find model letters to keep in a file for reference.	( )	( )
2. Put key points in capital letters so they stand out.	( )	( )
3. Stick to using only a few different fonts in one document.	( )	( )
4. Use little or no jargon or clichés in your writing.	( )	( )
5. Use the same words repeatedly to make your writing easy to read.	( )	( )

P R A C T I C E

Put the following items in the correct box as "good in writing" or "bad in writing."

bias	capital letters	facts	feedback	headers	humor
jargon	links	models	punctuation	references	slang

GOOD	BAD

Answer Key

Chapter 1. English for the Telephone

1. What makes a good telephone call? - p. 9

Dialog
plan / cold call / small talk / busy signal

Vocabulary
1. dial tone   2. redial   3. busy signal
4. zip code   5. greet

Practice
1. a   2. a   3. c   4. d   5. d

2. Making a call - p. 11

Dialog
dial tone / directory / connect / transfer

Vocabulary
1. receiver   2. star key   3. pound key
4. hold button   5. cord

Practice
1. through   2. back   3. down   4. with   5. up

3. Switchboard speaking! - p. 13

Dialog
speak / leave / meeting / call you back

Vocabulary
1. colleague 2. answer 3. line 4. identify 5. sorry

Practice
1. b   2. d   3. e   4. c   5. a

4. Opening a call - p. 15

Dialog
reason / check / give / indigo

Vocabulary
1. b   2. d   3. a   4. b   5. d

Practice
1. Edward/echo, apple/alpha, Robert/Romeo
2. jacket/Juliet, Edward/echo, Robert/Romeo, Robert/Romeo, yes/yellow
3. summer/sierra, apple/alpha, go/golf, Edward/echo
4. yes/yellow, Edward/echo, summer/sierra
5. day/delta, apple/alpha, window/whiskey

5. Receiving and taking messages - p. 17

Dialog
number / Go ahead / make sure / tell

Vocabulary
date / name / message / action

Practice
1. d   2. b   3. e   4. c   5. a

6. Structuring a call - p. 19

Dialog
confirm / get back to you / leave it to / organize

Vocabulary
1. b   2. e   3. c   4. a   5. d

Practice
1. deflecting   2. checking
3. telling the purpose
4. deciding   5. ending

7. Transferring information - p. 21

Dialog
Excuse me / important / information / read that back

Vocabulary
1. c   2. e   3. a   4. b   5. d

Practice
1. start   2. catch   3. go over   4. check   5. respond

8. Communication difficulties - p. 23

Dialog
busy / hardly / hang up / wrong number

Vocabulary
1. a   2. c   3. b   4. e   5. d

Practice
1. a   2. c   3. b   4. d   5. c

9. Calling back - p. 25

Dialog
returning / getting back to / available / call you back

Vocabulary
1. restarting   2. opening   3. giving an excuse
4. thanking   5. giving a reason

Practice
5 - 4 - 2 - 1 - 3

10. Making appointments - p. 27

Dialog
schedule / convenient / planner / ideal

Vocabulary
1. c   2. d   3. e   4. b   5. a

Practice
check / meet / reschedule / pick up / postponed

11. Complaining - p. 29

Dialog
apologize / oversight / immediately / inconvenieuce

Vocabulary
1. receive   2. damage   3. repair
4. promise   5. request

Practice
1. received   2. as soon as possible
3. unacceptable   4. responsibility
5. a clerical error

12. Closing a call - p. 31

Dialog
go over / leave it at / patience / assistance

Vocabulary
1. transfer   2. organize   3. receiver
4. trip   5. grateful

Practice
1. c   2. a   3. e   4. d   5. b

13. Cross-cultural tips/Audio conferencing - p. 33

Dialog
directness / appropriate / guarantee / clarify

Vocabulary
1. d   2. c   3. b   4. e   5. a

Practice
1. punctuality   2. directness   3. humor
4. silence   5. small talk

14. Golden rules - p. 35

Dialog
referred to / aggressive / anticipate / representing

Vocabulary
1. DO   2. DON'T   3. DON'T   4. DO   5. DO

Practice
1. a   2. b   3. a   4. c   5. b

Chapter 2. English for Presentations

1. What makes a good presentation? - p. 39

Dialog
adjust / allotted / structure / eye contact

Vocabulary
1. d   2. b   3. c   4. e   5. a

Practice
questions / introduction / greeting / main
points / conclusion

2. Starting - p. 41

Dialog
title / outline / points / brief

Vocabulary
1. springboard   2. comment   3. persuade
4. divide   5. in-depth

Practice
1. position   2. title
3. overhead projector/OHP
4. brief   5. convince

3. Signaling - linking the parts - p. 43

Dialog
ideas / questions / deal with / come back to

Vocabulary
1. e   2. d   3. a   4. b   5. c

Practice
1. a   2. a   3. a   4. d   5. c

4. Highlighting and emphasizing - p. 45

Dialog
remarkable / Frankly / essential / reiterate

Vocabulary
1. totally   2. carefully   3. repeatedly
4. exactly   5. basically

Practice
1. work   2. absolute   3. far too
4. simply   5. dramatic

5. Engaging your audience - p. 47

Dialog
point of view / diplomatic / show of hands /
acknowledge

Vocabulary
1. to spend more time   2. for a show of hands
3. for clarification   4. a rhetorical question
5. to see statistics

Practice
1. b   2. d   3. b   4. d   5. a

6. Visual aids — design and type - p. 49

Dialog
illustrate / first glance / diagram / color

Vocabulary
1. bar chart   2. table   3. pie chart
4. flow chart   5. diagram

Practice
1. compatible   2. layout   3. distracted
4. technical

7. Visual aids — describing charts - p. 51

Dialog
slump / recovered / deterioration / low point

Vocabulary
1. stable   2. decrease   3. fluctuate
4. rocket   5. improve

Practice
1. fall   2. recovery   3. rise   4. fluctuation   5. peak

8. Body language — being persuasive - p. 53

Dialog
proposal / enthusiastic / posture / facial

Vocabulary
1. c   2. a   3. d   4. b   5. e

Practice
1. b   2. d   3. b   4. c   5. d

9. Communicating styles - p. 55

Dialog
exaggerating / utilize / in-depth / balanced

Vocabulary
1. d   2. c   3. a   4. e   5. b

Practice
1. informal   2. formal   3. informal
4. formal   5. informal

10. Closing a presentation - p. 57

Dialog
summarize / conclude / attention / invite

Vocabulary
1. ...advised the...   2. ...go over these...
3. ...recommendation of...
4. ...final point...   5. ...handouts of...

Practice
1. d   2. c   3. b   4. e   5. a

11. Handling questions - p. 59

■ **Dialog**
difficult / hedging / depend on / follow

■ **Vocabulary**
1. d   2. c   3. a   4. e   5. b

■ **Practice**
1. d   2. c   3. d   4. b   5. a

12. Presenting at a glance - p. 61

■ **Dialog**
greeting / body / digress / handled

■ **Vocabulary**
1. Body   2. Introduction 3. Ending
4. Introduction 5. Ending

■ **Practice**
1. d   2. e   3. c   4. b   5. a

13. Cross-cultural tips - p. 63

■ **Dialog**
bear with me / specific / interrupt / contribute

■ **Vocabulary**
1. suitable   2. dynamic   3. sufficient
4. irrelevant   5. rigid

■ **Practice**
1. dress code   2. spontaneity   3. hierarchy
4. lack   5. punctuality

14. Golden rules - p. 65

■ **Dialog**
distracting / anecdotes / appropriate /
spontaneity

■ **Vocabulary**
1. DO 2. DON'T 3. DON'T 4. DO 5. DON'T

■ **Practice**
Good points:
1. established 2. sufficient   3. preparation
Bad points:
1. blocked   2. volume

Chapter 3 English for Meetings

1. What makes a good meeting? - p. 69

■ **Dialog**
circulating / attend / propose / refreshments

■ **Vocabulary**
1. c   2. d   3. e   4. b   5. a

■ **Practice**
agenda / combination / propose / positive /
attend

2. Meetings: key terms - p. 71

■ **Dialog**
recommendations / nominate / writes up /
adjourns

■ **Vocabulary**
1. break 2. proposal 3. point 4. matters 5. kick off

■ **Practice**
1. c   2. e   3. a   4. d   5. b

3. Opening a meeting - p. 73

■ **Dialog**
absence / target / go around / take minutes

■ **Vocabulary**
1. c   2. e   3. a   4. d   5. b

■ **Practice**
1. ...meeting to less...   2. ...background about...
3. ...allocated each...   4. ...minute-taker...
5. ...her apologies...

4. Giving and responding to opinions - p. 75

■ **Dialog**
comment / extent / negatively / hear from

■ **Vocabulary**
1. disagree   2. disagree   3. disagree
4. agree   5. agree

■ **Practice**
1. c   2. c   3. d   4. b   5. c

5. Controlling - p. 77

■ **Dialog**
reformulate / side-tracked / scope / move on

■ **Vocabulary**
1. d   2. b   3. a   4. e   5. c

■ **Practice**
1. motivate   2. come to   3. reformulate
4. clarify   5. skip

6. Interruptions - p. 79

■ **Dialog**
add / superficially / in more depth / at once

■ **Vocabulary**
1. at once   2. interrupt   3. in more depth
4. relevant   5. exploit

■ **Practice**
1. b   2. d   3. c   4. a   5. e

7. Asking questions - p. 81

■ **Dialog**
elaborate / vital / with me / thoroughly

■ **Vocabulary**
1. CLOSED   2. OPEN   3. CLOSED
4. CLOSED   5. OPEN

■ **Practice**
1. repeat   2. repeat   3. clarify
4. elaborate 5. clarify

8. Making decisions - p. 83

■ **Dialog**
out of time / consensus / reject / carries

■ **Vocabulary**
1. put on 2. consensus 3. rejected 4. defer 5. focus

■ **Practice**
1. d   2. c   3. d   4. a   5. a

9. Closing a meeting - p. 85

■ **Dialog**
sum up / minutes / contribution / productive

■ **Vocabulary**
1. informal   2. adjourned   3. constructive
4. stimulating 5. pointless

■ **Practice**
1. d   2. a   3. b   4. c   5. e

10. Problem-solving meetings - p. 87

■ **Dialog**
arose / tackle / postpone / anticipate

■ **Vocabulary**
1. technical   2. communication
3. time   4. financial   5. manpower

■ **Practice**
1. d   2. c   3. b   4. a   5. c

11. Vocabulary building - p. 89

■ **Dialog**
objective / unanimous / implement / hasty

■ **Vocabulary**
1. e   2. a   3. d   4. c   5. b

■ **Practice**
1. forward   2. out   3. up   4. with   5. to

12. Meetings at a glance - p. 91

■ **Dialog**
opinion / stuck to it / prepared / running
over time

■ **Vocabulary**
1. objective   2. points of view
3. ideas   4. decision   5. date

■ **Practice**
1. summarize   2. partly   3. for taking
4. could cover   5. further

13. Cross-cultural tips - p. 93

■ **Dialog**
diplomacy / behave / offend / business cards

■ **Vocabulary**
1. individually   2. organically   3. collectively
4. systematically 5. silently

■ **Practice**
1. a   2. d   3. b   4. b   5. a

14. Golden rules - p. 95

■ **Dialog**
organize / guarantees / authority / dominate

■ **Vocabulary**
1. DON'T   2. DON'T   3. DO   4. DO   5. DO

■ **Practice**
1. agenda   2. name cards   3. conference room
4. minutes   5. refreshments

Chapter 4 English for Socializing

1. First meetings - p. 99

■ **Dialog**
free / catch / look around / miserable

■ **Vocabulary**
1. person   2. wonderful   3. manage
4. calm   5. early

■ **Practice**
1. e   2. b   3. a   4. d   5. c

2. Social phrases — responding - p. 101

■ **Dialog**
take a break / mind / shame / annoying

■ **Vocabulary**
1. b   2. c   3. e   4. a   5. d

■ **Practice**
1. hasn't got a clue   2. matters
3. never mind   4. typical   5. give a hand

3. Talking about jobs - p. 103

■ **Dialog**
applying for / freelance / salaries / stressful

■ **Vocabulary**
Boss: Alice
Sales Manager: Charles
Office Manager: Tom
Sales Reps: Nancy / Mary

■ **Practice**
1. a   2. c   3. d   4. b   5. d

4. Talking about family and relationships - p. 105

■ **Dialog**
married / separated / dating / remarry

■ **Vocabulary**
1. sister-in-law   2. aunt   3. grandfather
4. nephew   5. cousin

■ **Practice**
The answers will vary.

5. Talking about home - p. 107

■ **Dialog**
suburbs / region / surrounded by / mortgage

■ **Vocabulary**
1. kitchen   2. yard   3. living room
4. bedroom   5. bathroom

■ **Practice**
1. house / carpet / fireplace / kitchen
2. overlooking / tiled

6. Talking about interests and sport - p. 109

■ **Dialog**
free time / courts / tournament / courses

■ **Vocabulary**
1. a   2. c   3. b   4. e   5. d

■ **Practice**
spectators / Stadium / field / referee / tie

7. Talking about movies and stage shows - p. 111

■ **Dialog**
premier / lead / reviews / performance

■ **Vocabulary**
1. subtitles   2. star   3. soundtrack
4. hero   5. climax

■ **Practice**
1. performance   2. reserved   3. aisle
4. row   5. seat

8. Talking about vacations - p. 113

■ **Dialog**
camping / quaint / touristy / cabin

■ **Vocabulary**
1. d   2. e   3. a   4. c   5. b
■ **Practice**
1. c   2. b   3. a   4. a   5. a

9. Talking about business environment - p. 115
■ **Dialog**
recession / unemployment / downsize / outsourcing
■ **Vocabulary**
1. downsizing   2. falling market
3. inflation   4. unbalanced trade
5. high unemployment
■ **Practice**
1. interest   2. take over   3. booming
4. merged with   5. joint venture

10. Talking about health and lifestyle - p. 117
■ **Dialog**
come down with / food poisoning /
diagnosed / prescription
■ **Vocabulary**
1. bruise   2. cholesterol   3. hangover
4. temperature   5. sore
■ **Practice**
suffering from / sore throat / knocked
unconscious / heart attack / diagnosed

11. Making invitations - p. 119
■ **Dialog**
wondering / delighted / recommended /
looking forward to
■ **Vocabulary**
1. ACCEPT   2. DECLINE   3. DECLINE
4. ACCEPT   5. DECLINE
■ **Practice**
1. predicting the number   2. offering an invitation
3. explaining formality   4. giving directions
5. setting the time

12. Eating out - p. 121
■ **Dialog**
delicious / tasty / vegetarian / wine
■ **Vocabulary**
1. Starters   2. Main Course 3. Grill
4. Wine list   5. Desserts
■ **Practice**
1. b   2. a   3. b   4. c   5. c

13. Saying good-bye - p. 123
■ **Dialog**
miss / pleasure / appreciate / keep in touch
■ **Vocabulary**
1. c   2. d   3. a   4. e   5. b
■ **Practice**
1. ...borrow yours...   2. ...about thirty...
3. ...have a good...   4. ...departing...
5. ...need to confirm..

14. Cross-cultural tips - p. 125
■ **Dialog**
behavior / hierarchy / sensitivity / stereotype

■ **Vocabulary**
1. small talk   2. dress code
3. facial expressions   4. personal space
5. eye contact
■ **Practice**
1. Professionalism   2. Honesty
3. Punctuality   4. Directness   5. Hospitality

Chapter 5 English for Negotiating

1. What makes a successful negotiation? - p. 129
■ **Dialog**
procedure / initially / extend / bargaining
■ **Vocabulary**
1. advantage   2. priority   3. timetable
4. expectation   5. strategy
■ **Practice**
1. e   2. d   3. b   4. a   5. c

2. The negotiator and key terms - p. 131
■ **Dialog**
settlement / confident / established / haggle
■ **Vocabulary**
1. e   2. a   3. b   4. c   5. d
■ **Practice**
1. PROGRESS   2. PROGRESS
3. NO PROGRESS   4. PROGRESS
5. NO PROGRESS

3. Opening — creating the right climate - p. 133
■ **Dialog**
colleague / offer / took over / full
■ **Vocabulary**
1. using small talk   2. greeting
3. offering   4. welcoming   5. introducing
■ **Practice**
1. Really? That's interesting.
2. Ten degrees below zero!
3. Yes, I traveled to Germany.
4. No. Do you?
5. Me too!

4. Agreeing on an agenda - p. 135
■ **Dialog**
drawn up / concentrate on / sitting in / at this
point
■ **Vocabulary**
1. a   2. d   3. e   4. c   5. b
■ **Practice**
1. c   2. b   3. b   4. a   5. c

5. Opening statements — stating your position
- p. 137
■ **Dialog**
profile / brochures / stress / priority
■ **Vocabulary**
1. accordingly   2. currently   3. chiefly
4. frequently   5. immediately
■ **Practice**
1. X   2. O   3. X   4. X   5. O

6. Clarifying positions - p. 139

■ **Dialog**
require / minimum / sympathetic / secondary

■ **Vocabulary**
1. ... looking at...   2. ... took into account...
3. ... move on to...   4. ...depends on three...
5. ...had in mind...

■ **Practice**
3 - 4 - 1 - 2 - 5

7. Making and responding to proposals - p. 141

■ **Dialog**
point of view / alternative / propose / respond

■ **Vocabulary**
1. POSITIVE   2. NEGATIVE   3. NEUTRAL
4. POSITIVE   5. NEUTRAL

■ **Practice**
1. b   2. b   3. c   4. d   5. a

8. Bargaining - p. 143

■ **Dialog**
reiterate / acceptable / proviso / deal

■ **Vocabulary**
1. c   2. b   3. d   4. a   5. e

■ **Practice**
1. accepting   2. rejecting
3. setting condition 4. setting condition
5. making new offer

9. Handling conflict and resolving sticking points - p. 145

■ **Dialog**
common ground / overcome / demands / obstacles

■ **Vocabulary**
1. unable   2. objection   3. encounter
4. mutual   5. detail

■ **Practice**
1. reassure you 2. come back   3. requested
4. maintained   5. cool down

10. Closing a negotiation - p. 147

■ **Dialog**
go over / legal / agreement / suits

■ **Vocabulary**
1. b   2. e   3. d   4. a   5. c

■ **Practice**
1. d   2. a   3. c   4. d   5. a

11. Negotiation — an overview - p. 149

■ **Dialog**
background / basis / factor / got started

■ **Vocabulary**
1. major   2. clarify   3. objective
4. reasonable 5. remains

■ **Practice**
1. b   2. d   3. c   4. e   5. a

12. Phrasal verbs and idioms for negotiating - p. 151

■ **Dialog**
bogged down / give ground / worked out /
up my sleeve

■ **Vocabulary**
1. a   2. c   3. f   4. b   5. e   6. d

■ **Practice**
1. play by ear   2. carry on
3. reach a stalemate
4. rush into   5. give in

13. Cross-cultural tips - p. 153

■ **Dialog**
proposition / briefed / adapt / tactics

■ **Vocabulary**
1. Japanese   2. Japanese
3. British   4. American, Latin
5. American   6. American

■ **Practice**
1. a   2. d   3. b   4. c   5. d

14. Golden rules - p. 155

■ **Dialog**
psychology / sensitive / identified / package

■ **Vocabulary**
1. ...is complex
2. ...global perspective
3. ...positive personalities
4. ...is valuable
5. ...is not consistent

■ **Practice**
1. DON'T 2. DO   3. DO   4. DON'T 5. DO

Chapter 6 Writing for International Business: E-mails, Letters and Reports

1. Successful writing - p. 159

■ **Dialog**
pay attention / content / key point / concise

■ **Vocabulary**
1. a   2. b   3. b   4. d   5. a

■ **Practice**
1. e   2. d   3. b   4. c   5. a

2. Organizing information - p. 161

■ **Dialog**
sort out / brainstorm / practical / report

■ **Vocabulary**
1. pyramid   2. chronology   3. process
4. chronology   5. pyramid

■ **Practice**
1. decide objective of writing
2. brainstorm
3. choose method of organization
4. outline report
5. fill in details

3. The Business letter — layout - p. 163

■ **Letter**
intended / adequate / standard / Sincerely

■ **Vocabulary**
1. d   2. c   3. a   4. b   5. e

Practice
1. consistent   2. justified   3. standard
4. optional   5. adequate

4. Correspondence phrases - p. 165

Letter
grateful / apologize / enclosing / contact

Vocabulary
1. b   2. c   3. a   4. e   5. d

Practice
1. E-MAIL   2. LEGAL CONTRACT
3. REPORT   4. LEGAL CONTRACT
5. E-MAIL

5. Model letters - p. 167

Letter
confirm / hold / payment / convenient

Vocabulary
1. e   2. b   3. d   4. a   5. c

Practice
1. accepting   2. requesting   3. explaining
4. complaining   5. confirming

6. Writing clearly — extra points - p. 169

Letter
jargon / consistent / captions / absolutely

Vocabulary
1. cliché   2. reprimand   3. justified
4. dynamic   5. option

Practice
1. c   2. b   3. a   4. a   5. a

7. The business report — layout - p. 171

Report
investigation / feedback / recommendations / appendices

Vocabulary
1. indentation   2. deadline   3. background
4. title   5. scope

Practice
1. c   2. d   3. e   4. a   5. b

8. Connecting words - p. 173

Report
effective / efficiency / bring about / above-mentioned

Vocabulary
1. In addition   2. In particular   3. For example
4. However   5. Therefore

Practice
First / This / and / Second / especially

9. E-mail - p. 175

E-mail
attachment / print / personal / retrieving

Vocabulary
1. b   2. a   3. d   4. e   5. c

Practice
1. d   2. a   3. a   4. a   5. d

10. The perfect résumé - p. 177

Dialog
well-structured / tailor / accomplishments / attract

Vocabulary
1. c   2. a   3. e   4. b   5. d

Practice
1. Objective   2. Education
3. Work Experience
4. Skills   5. References

11. Grammar and spelling check - p. 179

Dialog
reputation / rely on / non-essential / advice

Vocabulary
1. AMERICAN   2. BRITISH   3. BRITISH
4. AMERICAN   5. BRITISH

Practice
1. ...data correctly...
2. ...has been researching...
3. ...negotiation are...
4. ...fax arrived...
5. ...must be...

12. Punctuation - p. 181

Dialog
punctuation / commas / break / colon

Vocabulary
1. ... team, you...
2. ...deadline, we...
3. ...beautiful, but...
4. ...coffee, tea, muffins, and...
5. Bob, who manages the sales department, has...

Practice
(Answers will vary.)
1. My full name is Linda Strait.
2. My nationality is American.
3. I was born on November 16, 1955.
4. I can speak English and French.
5. I would like to live in Bangkok, Thailand.

13. Getting technical - p. 183

Manual
critical / technical / initiate / press

Vocabulary
1. content   2. permit   3. volume
4. complain of   5. immobilize

Practice
1. d   2. d   3. c   4. a   5. c

14. Golden rules - p. 185

Dialog
re-drafted / logically / emphasizes / keep in mind

Vocabulary
1. DO   2. DON'T   3. DO   4. DO   5. DON'T

Practice
GOOD - facts, feedback, headers, links, models, punctuation, references, capital letters
BAD - bias, humor, jargon, slang